Successful Parenting

Successful Parenting

by Ann M. Murphy, Ed. M.
and John F. Murphy, Ed. M.

ST. PAUL EDITIONS

NIHIL OBSTAT:
    Rev. Richard V. Lawlor, S.J.
    Censor

IMPRIMATUR:
    ✤ Most Rev. Thomas V. Daily
    October 7, 1983

Library of Congress Cataloging in Publication Data

Murphy, Ann M.
    Successful parenting.

    1. Parenting. 2. Parenting—Religious aspects. I. Murphy, John F. II. Title.
HQ755.8.M875   1983   306.8'74   83-15290

ISBN 0-8198-6841-8 c
     0-8198-6842-6 p

Printed in the U.S.A. by the Daughters of St. Paul
50 St. Paul's Ave., Boston, MA 02130

The Daughters of St. Paul are an international congregation of religious women serving the Church with the communications media.

This book is dedicated to
Rev. A. Paul White, Editor of *The Pilot*

CONTENTS

Acknowledgments 13
Preface 17
Children and Television 21
The World of "Less Tall" Folk! 27
Fighting Within the Home 33
The Many Faces of Friendship 39
A Christmas Prayer 45
Talk to Your Children About God 51
Vacation Time and Home Alone 59
Mothers and Daughters 65
Is Your Child Spoiled? 73
They Called Him a Dreamer 81
Guilt Is Like a Black Crayon Mark 87
Handling Mid-Life Crisis 93
The Power of Touch 99
Grandpa's Philosophy 105
Help for the Shy Child 111
For Fathers—On Fathers' Day 117
For Mothers—On Mothers' Day 123
Do You Have Trouble Sleeping? 129
Is Silence Helpful in Family Life? 137
The Pain and Trauma of Divorce 143
Turning Things Around
    for the Rocky Marriage 151

Let Music Be an Important Part
     of Living 157
The Pain and Sting of a Put-Down 165
And Now It Is Lent 171
Volunteer Your Time and Talents 177
Talk to Your Teenagers
     About Responsible Driving 183
Getting Children To Help
     Around the House 189
What Is Love? 197
"I Must Set You Free" 203
A Closer Look at Drugs and Alcohol ... 209
Have You Taught Your Children
     the Facts of Life? 217
Baby-sitters Are Important People! 225
They Also Deserve Forgiveness... 233
Exciting Expressions! 241
They March to the Tune
     of New Pipers 247
Let's Close Some Doors! 253

Acknowledgments

We have many people and organizations to thank as we assemble the chapters of this book. Without their acceptance, help and inspiration, our thoughts would be shallow and our pages would be blank.

First, we would like to say "thank you" and "we love you" to our son, John, and our daughter, Mary Ellen. Raising them was truly an exciting and rewarding experience. They are now grown and on their way in the world, but during their growing up years, together we slowly, happily—and sometimes painfully—learned the lessons written here within.

Thank you, too, to our parents; Margaret and Leo Hickey, and "Meme" and John Murphy. As children, we sometimes disagreed with them, but their love kept us together, through the happy times and the rough times as well.

We extend our heartfelt thanks to Rev. A. Paul White, Editor of *The Pilot* (to whom this book is dedicated) and to his wonderful staff who have faithfully printed our parenting column each week in their newspaper. They gave us strength "to keep on writing," even when the fingers were very weary! And, the friendship and professional expertise of Drs. John and Eunice Gilmore have been and continue to be extremely valuable to us. Their wise counsel contributed very considerably to our personal understanding of what it means to be "a good parent."

We are indebted to Rev. Frank McFarland and Jack Lawless of The Boston Catholic Television Center; they helped us organize, video-tape and air 55 Successful Parenting cable television programs. Others who have generously given us assistance include: The Benedictine Monks of Glastonbury Abbey, Hingham, MA; the Catholic Press Association, who kindly honored us with their journalism award; Rev. Michael McGarry and the Paulist Center in Boston; Dr. Leo Donahue and the St. Vincent De Paul Society; and Jay Asher and the staff of radio station WJDA, Quincy, MA.

Other organizations have also helped us learn, write and lecture about parenting. They are: The Council for Exceptional Children; The Massachusetts Association for Children with Learning Disabilities; Massachusetts Title I Parents and Children; the many religious and secular publications throughout the United States and

Canada who print our "Successful Parenting" column; The Parent Counseling Association of New England; The Plymouth County Teachers Association; Fitchburg State College; The Hingham Public Schools; the many parishes of the Archdiocese of Boston; church groups, schools and community organizations throughout New England.

In thinking back over the years, we remain forever grateful to two men in the field of education who encouraged our early writing and speaking endeavors. They are Professor James J. St. Germain of our Alma Mater, Merrimack College, North Andover, MA, and Brother Timothy Linus of Central Catholic High School, Lawrence, MA.

Finally, a very special thank you to our publishers, the Daughters of St. Paul! One day their letter arrived to tell us that they had accepted this—our first book—for publication. We were delighted! *Successful Parenting* is a collection of newspaper columns which originated with *The Pilot,* the newspaper for the Archdiocese of Boston, published by our late beloved Cardinal Humberto Medeiros, Archbishop of Boston.

We hope these chapters will help you and your children become united in peace and joy and love. God bless you all!

Ann and John Murphy

Preface

What does it mean to be a good parent? How can parents be successful in raising children? "Am I doing the right thing?" These are the questions which many parents are asking today.

We would like to share our parenting research, methods, and philosophy with you. We realize that mothers and fathers face tremendous challenges today. Raising children can be exciting and rewarding; however, sometimes it becomes frightening and frustrating. Children are vulnerable to parents' thoughts, words, and actions. However, when parents become positive in their outlook, loving in their attitude, and kind in their actions, then raising boys and girls can become a most rewarding, worthwhile, lifetime accomplishment.

We have read study after study which explains that we must begin with basics with children. The beginning road to becoming a good parent, therefore, is to begin with Basic Rule Number I, and that is "Love." Showing children love by replacing criticism in the home with kind words of praise, encouragement, and approval is where parents must begin. Then follow this up with hugs, kisses, kind spoken words, lots of listening, and written notes to children. This all builds self-esteem in children and helps them realize they are important because they are loved.

Good parenting also involves effective discipline and helping children become successful in school and successful with social responsibilities. It means rules and standards for good moral behavior, for television watching, and for money management. Children need help with developing hobbies, interests, careers, and last but not least, a sense of humor.

Parents who have become involved in this positive, developmental approach to parenting have noticed some exciting results happening within their homes. Their home environment has become more loving, caring and kind. The nagging, fighting and bickering disappear. Mothers and fathers, including those who are single parents, have told us that their children have become happier, more hopeful, and healthier.

As you read the following chapters about these methods which we call "Building Steps for Successful Parenting," we hope you will try them out in your own homes.

We agree with the poet Powell:

Who we are,
Who we become,
    is determined
    by those
Who love us.

1

Children and Television

"We don't allow any television watching in our house!"

"TV is a monster in our world today!"

"Our children watch all the television they want; it doesn't hurt them."

Statements of this kind are heard in the homes of many families today. The views about the good effects versus the bad effects of television are debated and discussed so frequently that many parents, teachers, and children become bewildered in the maze of controversy. Some parents absolutely refuse to allow a television set in their homes, while other parents and children watch TV morning, noon, and night. Then, there are the moderates who watch occasionally; they sample, they sip, and they wonder and worry about the effects of television on growing children.

When we become honest with ourselves, most of us would admit the lure of this so-called monster. It tempts us and we watch our own favorite shows: the news, a comedy show, a drama, a game show, a cartoon, a television documentary, a soap opera, and even a humorous commercial. We don't feel guilty about this; in fact, many times it helps us to relax and to forget some of the problems of our day-to-day routines. It also makes us curious about certain subjects and often sends us to the library to read and to learn about a new world which television has introduced to us.

Have you ever heard an excellent speaker on television and said to yourself, "I'd love to be able to talk like him or her!" Or, have you ever seen a talented dancer, comedian, or musician and thought, "Someday I'm going to learn to do that, too!" Yes, we feel that television can inspire children and adults when it provides worthwhile role-models to emulate.

Television can be our special window, opened wide to look out upon the whole world. We can sit in our living room or prop ourselves up in bed and see the President visiting foreign countries, the Pope journeying to all parts of the world, and kings and queens traveling to distant lands. Is it a terrible monster or a teaching master when it reveals spewing volcanoes, whirling blizzards, storming seas, and parched deserts? Is it a wicked wasteland or a wonderous wizard when it thrills us with the beauties in nature: the flower gardens, the snow-topped mountains, the jungle waterfalls, the forest animals, and the fish in the sea?

The attraction of television and its effects upon children will most likely be debated for a long time. It is like comparing watermelons and grapefruits, sweet fruits and bitter fruits, goodness and evil. Perhaps what we should be discussing here is not television at all. Few of us own television stations; few of us are television producers, and although we can write letters to protest the evils of this medium, our views are often not considered. What appears to be the issue is not television, but rather temptation...the temptation which constantly flirts with our time and how we spend our time and whether we will say "on" or dare to say "off" to that TV control switch.

Do we give in to temptation when we should be working, planning, or playing with our children? Can we say "yes" to the worthwhile shows on television and "no" to the obscene, materialistic, mindless trash which spills itself into our living rooms? Can we stand tall and firm and turn off that TV when it tempts our youngsters with false values, illicit sexual behavior, and violence?

Do we know what our sons and daughters are watching on television? Let's ask them; let's sit down and talk about it. Maybe we will all learn something to discuss and to debate.

2

The World of "Less Tall" Folk!

Today we ask you to sit back in your chair, close your eyes and think about the days—so long ago and far away—when you were quite young. You probably had freckles on your nose and a missing front tooth. When you looked up at your Mom and Dad, they appeared to be so tall; literally, you had to stand on tip-toes to reach the kitchen sink!

You were too young to play baseball with the big guys, too small to ride a two-wheel bike and too scared to stay alone in the house after dark. But you could crouch on the sidewalk for almost an hour and carefully study an army of ants as they carried crumbs from your peanut butter sandwich into their ant hole. Once in a while you would throw some twigs in their tracks; it was thrilling to observe their treacherous climb over each stick and leaf!

On rainy days you ventured up into the attic—all by yourself—and you dressed up in Mom's old evening dresses or Dad's old pants.

You'd stand before the cracked mirror, among the dust and the cobwebs, and pretend you were a famous movie star. No one was watching, so it was all right to sing and dance and make crazy faces at that funny little guy or gal in the dusty old mirror.

When the sun came out, it was always great fun to ride your red tricycle up and down the bumpy sidewalk. Your older brother or sister taught you how to count to "10," and you felt so grown up and proud as you counted all the lines on the sidewalk and marveled at the way your wheels could crush each one of them.

What else made you happy? Did you slide down giant slides, ride the merry-go-round until you were quite dizzy and go swinging high in the air on the playground swing? Did you ride see-saws and get scared and excited —at the same time—when some fresh guy made your end stay up and you couldn't jump down?

Did you play jump rope and marbles? Did you collect dolls and teddy bears and puppets?

Perhaps you had a special spot in the cellar where your Dad gave you all his extra nails and broken pieces of wood. You owned a small brown hammer and you would create boats and airplanes and creations which had no names at all. Some were quite long, others were small, but they were great vehicles for travel. And, in your five- or six- or seven-year-old mind, you frequently jumped aboard these wondrous machines and journeyed throughout the world. You were the captain; you were the crew!

Water always held a certain mystery and magic charm. Puddles in the backyard were your lakes for sailing small boats, they were your cuisine restaurant for concocting the finest mud pies in town, and they were the watering holes for your imaginary horse that carried you about each day.

Sometimes, after a rainstorm, you would run outside and watch the water run down the driveway! It seemed to flow like a mighty river! Quickly, you would gather clumps of grass and leaves and dam up the gushing flow. Then it would collect all around you. Your shoes became very wet and the dam weakened and broke. You jumped up and down, cheering the water as it pushed the dam aside and continued on its course to the street below.

Most likely, if you are still reading along here, you realize that your childhood was a special time indeed! But, why was it different? Why was it so grand? The answer is as simple as ABC...*you had time to play!*

Playing and using one's imagination is a wonderful way to grow and to learn and to have fun! Remember the old song: "Slide down my rain barrel, slide down my cellar door" (or something like that) "and we'll be jolly friends, forevermore!"

Now, you are older, wiser, taller and more serious, but it is still important to "take time for play!"

And don't forget your children; they like to play, too!

3

Fighting
Within the Home

The words we use in our families can either bind us closely together or tear us miserably apart. The way we listen and respond to those around us—especially those at home—is a vital part of family living.

Angry words, sarcasm, pouting, screaming and swearing are not solutions to family problems. Indeed, they only cause more trouble, more problems. Therefore, in response to many requests concerning "fighting within the home," we offer the following suggestions for mothers, fathers and children. We hope that these ideas will help you and your sons and daughters become happier, healthier and more understanding of one another.

First, let us consider the statement: "Don't be so fresh!" Why did Mom say that? What did Billy do? This is the way it happened:

Scene I   The Stolen Watch

(Billy, age eight, races home from school. He stomps into the kitchen and begins to cry.)

Billy: Somebody stole my new watch!

Mom: Are you sure you didn't lose it?

Billy: I didn't! I put it in my lunch box and now it's not there!

Mom: I told you to keep it on your wrist all day! That watch cost a lot of money! You're always losing things, Billy! When are you going to listen to me!

Billy: Oh, shut up, Mom!

Mom: Don't be so fresh!

Have you ever wished that you could replay a scene in your life? How could Mom have handled this situation in a better way? Let's set the stage, re-write the lines and play it again! This time Mom realizes the value of listening, caring and helping. She does not jump in with angry questions and impatient advice.

Scene II   The Found Watch

Billy: Somebody stole my new watch!

Mom: Oh?

Billy: I left it in my lunch box when I went out to recess and somebody stole it!

Mom: Mmmm.

Billy: That's the second time this week that somebody took my stuff. They stole my ball yesterday!

Mom: Uhhh!

Billy: Oh! Wait a minute, I found it! I put it in my pocket when I came back from recess!

Mom: I see.... I'm glad you found it, Billy!

(Conclusion: When a parent is questioning and blaming, it is very difficult for a child to think clearly and constructively. However, when parents stay calm, a child has a chance to explore his own thoughts and feelings and arrive at his own solutions.)

Our second family drama concerns a child's feelings. In this case, why did Dad say: "I can't reason with you!"

Scene I   The Lost Cat

Susie: (crying) My cat, Sam, ran away. He's been gone for four weeks!

Dad: Oh, Honey, don't get so upset. Don't cry, he was a very old cat.

Susie: Wah! Wah!

Dad: Stop crying, Susie! I'll buy you another cat!

Susie: I don't want another kitty! I want Sam!

Dad: I don't know what to do.... I can't reason with you!

When parents urge a child to forget bad feelings, the child seems to get even more upset. However, when parents use empathy, kindness and caring, they are helping the child. And when we acknowledge sadness—without trying to push it away—we are truly helping the child.

Scene II   Sam, Susie's Cat

Susie: (crying) My cat, Sam, ran away. He's been gone for four weeks.

Dad: Oh! No! That's terrible, Susie.

Susie: He was my friend.

Dad: When we lose a friend, it really hurts.

Susie: He used to play with me every day.

Dad: You two really had fun together.

Susie: I combed his fur every day.

Dad: (Arm around Susie and walking along together.) You really cared about that cat.

The manner in which we respond to children can make a significant difference in our family environment. If we, as parents, can learn to listen, pause, think—and then respond—we are helping our sons and daughters in an extremely positive way.

Naturally, every problem is not easily solved. Sometimes, children do need firm words and some type of punishment. Indeed, effective discipline is an important part of being a successful parent.

Finally, we must realize that we can never completely eliminate all fighting within the home. However, if our goals are peace, love and happiness, we must learn to:

- patiently listen
- quietly think
- prayerfully ponder
- then, lovingly speak.

4

The Many Faces
of Friendship

How many friends do you and your children have? What kind of people are they? Do your friends add or detract from the quality of your life?

In raising children, it is important to teach them about the value of friendships. Our friends can either help us, hurt us or have no influence on our lives at all. Some may be milk-toast, neither hot nor cold individuals.

Do parents and children need friends in our high-technology world of today? Our automobiles, buses, subways and trains race us around; our televisions provide escape and fantasies; and our computer systems replace the minds of many workers. We are living in an age of machines, new inventions, jet aircraft and space missions.

At times these master machines appear to dwarf and frighten us. We may question, "Do people need people anymore?" We would like to state clearly and firmly that these marvels of the twentieth century would be useless and obsolete without the support and interactions of people.

Yes, despite all our technical advancement since the horse and carriage days, we still need one another—we all need friends. Have you thought about the quality of your friendships? As a young boy put it recently: "What kind of guys do you hang around with?"

Your mother or your grandmother probably told you at least once, "You are judged by the company you keep." And then you ran off to the local movie theater to munch popcorn and candy and you wondered, "What did she mean by that?"

By no means would we attempt to change Grandma's words. They are as true today as they were twenty-five years ago. "The company we keep"..."the friends we have"..."our interpersonal skills"...there are many ways to talk about friends.

We would like to explore the whole idea of friendships and try to discover the meaning of our relationships with other people. Your first friend was probably the boy next door. Who are your friends now? Are they helping you, hurting you or leaving no mark on you whatsoever?

1. *Sad Friends.* They are weeping and crying and constantly unhappy. Their uncle died, their children are sick, their cat ran away and their

canary has a cold! They moan and they groan. But, indeed, they need you. Comfort them and try to make them smile. But, remember, sadness is contagious! Don't allow their grief to make you a sad friend, too.

2. *Angry Friends*. They are angry with their boss, their spouse, their children and everyone in the political, economic and religious world! They recite long stories about how they have been mistreated, abused and neglected. These people need you, too. They need a sounding board for their anger. Listen to them and try to help them see the more pleasant side of life. Take a walk with them, buy some ice cream cones and teach them how to look for rainbows and sunshine!

3. *Boring Friends*. They have few interests. They hate their lives and *you are probably their only friend*. They need you. Smile at their stories which they have told you a hundred times before. Tell them that you like their necktie or lipstick or new car. Try to interest them in other people. Tell them some *new* stories in order to improve their conversation.

4. *Old Friends*. They are like exquisite china, rare paintings and fine wine. They improve with age; you treasure all the years that you have known them. They love you even when you lose your job, forget your wallet, cry at weddings and forget the punch line to a joke!

5. *New Friends.* They are a joy and a pleasure! They add excitement and mystery to your
life! What are they *really* like? What do they
do? What are their likes and dislikes? Can you
learn something new from them? You need new
friends; they can enrich your life tremendously!

6. *Exciting Friends.* They make you smile
and laugh and feel fancy free! You take long
walks with them, you talk until dawn with them,
you enjoy their company more than words can
tell! They tell you about faraway places, new
books, challenging ideas and their dreams for the
future. They make you wish that all your friends
were "exciting friends."

7. *Extraordinary Friends.* If you are lucky—
very lucky—you may someday have an Extraordinary Friend. This person will make you want to
grow and learn and study. Extraordinary Friends
can nourish, excite and enthuse you. *In their
presence you seem to be something better than you
ever thought you would be.* They help you find the
miracles that exist within you.

They dare to mention words such as "God"
and "Faith" and "Love." Let them teach you and
guide you. Treasure the time which they give to
you. For, under their influence you will never
again be as you were. They have the power to
inspire you. They have the grace within them to
make you pray for the day when—maybe—you
can be an Extraordinary Friend, too!

5

A Christmas Prayer

I knelt by my Christmas manger
And felt a warm, holy glow.
I watched Mary and Joseph and Jesus
And the animals there in the snow.

I prayed that the love of Lord Jesus
Would come to me, show me the way,
For Christmas is not always easy,
Especially on each Christmas day.

But, I knew that this holy season,
With love and forgiveness and hope,
Would give me the needed courage
To live and to pray and to cope.

I decided to become very thankful
For all that the Lord did bestow,
And as I knelt by my holy manger,
I knew that we reap what we sow.

My thoughts became prayers of thanksgiving,
To Jesus, our Savior, our Lord;

I thanked Him for all His creation,
Our families, our country, our God.

Yes, sometimes we're spent and we're weary,
We feel hopeless, depressed and quite lost.
But Jesus, the Babe in the manger,
Saves and protects with no cost.

So, thank You, O little Lord Jesus,
In Your manger, so sweet and so dear;
You remind us on each Christmas morning
That we've lived through another good year.

You've given us dear friends and neighbors,
You gave us the power to reach out,
To love one another in darkness,
To laugh and to smile and not pout.

You've endowed us with keys to Your kingdom,
If we remain strong and so true.
Thank You, oh, thank You, Lord Jesus,
For the promise of heaven, and You!

And if in our families we falter,
Or stumble or limp and fall down,
We need only to turn to You, Jesus:
Your love and forgiveness abound!

I've knelt many hours by my manger,
On this cold, on this dreary, long day,
Brushing the tears from my eyelids,
And thanking the Lord as I pray.

I prayed for continuing guidance,
So that I might help, where I can;
I asked God in His infinite wisdom,
For patience, for answers, for plans.

For somewhere deep in the manger
Are solutions to all of our woe;
If families just love one another,
Our nation will prosper and grow.

Yes, thank You, oh, thank You, Lord Jesus,
For being that Babe in the hay;
Your gentle love will enfold us,
If only we follow Your way.

6

Talk to Your Children About God

Do you ever talk to your children about God? Does your young son or daughter picture God to be an old man who lives somewhere up in the sky, perhaps a cousin of Santa's, without the red suit? Do your teenagers question the existence of God, refusing to go to Mass, rejecting any belief in religion?

Certainly, when one attempts to write a chapter about children and their relationship to God, a writer becomes truly overwhelmed by the topic. And, indeed, troubling questions come to mind—questions such as: "How do I—myself—picture God?" "Should I study more philosophy and theology before even attempting this pursuit?" "Isn't it presumptuous for a person to speak or to write about a subject which is so difficult to comprehend, yet at the same time so dear to our hearts...so compelling and yet confusing?"

However, as parents we realize that religion, Christianity and moral living are the very core, the foundation of our lives here on earth. And, therefore, in order to impart these beliefs to our children, we feel that we should share, through our conversation and lifestyle, the feelings we have about God. Perhaps we are not always exact and maybe we cannot easily recite biblical chapters and verses, but if our intentions are to develop within our youngsters a love and trust in our Lord, we cannot afford to be silent.

Let us recall first some "echoes from the past." You may have heard a few of these twenty or thirty years ago. Our question is: "Is this the kind of religion which promotes love and trust and commitment?"

Echoes From the Past

1. "If you fight with your brother again, God will certainly punish you!"

2. "If God loves me," cried Jimmy, "why did He make it rain on my birthday?"

3. "Someone is lying!" screams Mom. "I can't tell who is telling the lie, but God can!"

4. "If you had been a good boy, God wouldn't have let you fall down and break your leg!"

What do you think about the previous statements? Do they instill in young children a love and trust in God? Is God to be perceived as a child abuser, as a non-loving Father, or as a stern judge? Should God be called upon to mediate arguments between children and parents?

When children misbehave—as they all do from time to time—the research indicates that it is far better for the parent to say: "Your behavior hurts and saddens me." Don't say, "Your behavior hurts God and He will punish it."

Also, try to explain to children that adversity (accidents, sickness and misfortune) affect both good and bad people. There are some mysteries about God which we will never completely understand until we "go to God" in heaven, and then He will make it all clear and true for us. Ask your children to have faith and patience. And then, remind your teenagers that there are few atheists in exam rooms, and fewer still on battlefields. Didn't you always pray before finals each semester?

Another topic regarding children and their relationship to God was recently mentioned by a first grader. "What does God look like?" she asked. Her mother thought a while and finally replied:

"I don't know, but I know He exists. Like the wind—sometimes, blowing and howling, other times, fanning and gently caressing us—we can't see the wind, but we can clearly see the work of the wind.

"God is like that, too," she continued. "We can't see God, but we can see men, women and children in our world, showing love and kindness to each other. And this is when we feel the presence of God among us."

Explain to your children that when there is mercy, patience and caring—then, God is there, too. Tell them stories about the Son of God, Jesus: the Babe of Bethlehem, the Man from Galilee, the long road to Jerusalem, and the empty tomb. God sent His Son almost two thousand years ago in order for us to better understand ourselves and to grow to love Him more. He became our Redeemer.

How do we deal with teenagers who doubt their faith, question your values and reject the Lord? Should you spend hours nagging, fighting, arguing and swearing at them because of their lack of religion? Can religion be forced upon young people?

Recent studies indicate that children, teenagers and young adults learn and develop their faith when parents:

- live their faith despite difficulties
- share their experiences (both good and bad) with their sons and daughters

- tell their children true stories about how their faith has sustained them.

Finally, what do we know about adults and their relationship to God? How clearly do any of us understand our Creator? Do you picture a grandfatherly Spirit in the sky with a long white beard, and a gentle, smiling face? What is your relationship with God?

As we stated at the beginning, this is truly an overwhelming subject, but it is a most worthwhile subject.... Perhaps you may wish to discuss it with your children at dinnertime tonight.

7

Vacation Time
and Home Alone

Summer vacation time! A time for swimming and playing and eating ice cream cones! The lazy, hazy, crazy days...reading and dreaming and picnicking under the willow tree...or sipping pink lemonade on the swinging hammock!

And then the thunder cracks, lightning streaks across the sky and the reality of living interrupts our lovely summer daydream. We see a young boy, about ten years old, home alone with seventy long days ahead of him. He is but one of the millions of children in this country who must take care of themselves during summer vacation. His Dad doesn't live with him anymore, and his Mom must work in order to support herself and her young son.

Many studies reveal that children worry that someone might break into their homes and harm them. They fear noises, darkness and loneliness. However, most boys and girls do not tell their parents about their anxieties. At a very tender age, they reason to themselves: "Mom or Dad have it hard enough. I don't want to bother anyone with my scary feelings."

The whole issue of "to work or not to work?"—especially for mothers—is an enormous question. There are thousands of single parents and married couples, too, who truly *must* work each day. It is a matter of economic or psychological survival. No one of us has a right to preach or to judge.

However, summer vacation days arrive each year, with crime and burglaries soaring to an all-time high. Research indicates that, with careful planning, parents can help children who have apprehensions about being alone. If you are faced with this dilemma, we hope that the following suggestions will help you and your children have a happier, safer summertime.

It's Summertime and the Living Is Scary

1. "I'm scared that someone will break in and hurt me." ...Install new safe locks on your doors. A few dollars spent on good locks will provide a better sense of security for both you and your child.

2. "When I'm home alone, I have no one to help me." ...Make sure that your child knows a few neighbors whom he or she can call upon in case of emergency.

3. "If something really bad happens, what should I do?" ...Tape police and fire department telephone numbers on your telephone. Explain to your child how to call these numbers if it is necessary.

4. "I wish I could talk to Mom and Dad during the day. I get lonesome." ...Make it a practice to telephone your child each day while you are at work. Whether children are ten, twelve or sixteen, it is good to keep in touch.

5. "I get so bored in the summertime." ...Plan visits to the homes of friends (preferably ones whose parents are home), trips to the library, daily chores, enrollment in recreation programs or music lessons.

6. "What should I do if I fall down and cut myself?" ...Prepare a safety kit with bandages, first aid materials and a small amount of money for emergency use only.

7. "I wish I had a dog or cat to keep me company." ...Why not?

8. "You're always late, Mom, where were you?" ...Try to get home on time. Arrive with a smile, a hug and a kiss. Remember, the *quality* of the time you spend with your child is what will be remembered.

Be firm, be fair, be consistent...and employ large amounts of laughter, love and kindness in your non-working hours.

8

Mothers and Daughters

"A boy for you, a girl for me!" The old-time song echoes in our memory! Let us explore the second half of this "Tea for Two" verse—namely, "a girl for me." We will take a careful look into the world of mother - daughter relationships. And, if you are a daughter, a mother, a grand-mother—or all three—or if you know any of these kinds of people (have we left anyone out?), then, you may agree that this is certainly an exciting and provocative topic.

From the moment of birth, through all the days of their lives, mothers and daughters must deal with emotional reactions toward one another—some positive, some negative.

As in all relationships, words are powerful factors in bringing us together or tearing us apart. "Another girl!" we often hear. "We were really wishing for a boy." These sentiments can have a profound effect upon daughters through-out infancy, childhood, teen years and adult-hood.

Another force which affects the mother-daughter bond is the whole issue of personality. Maybe Mom is a perfect lady and young Susie would rather play softball, climb trees and wallow in the mud. What happens? Can Mom adjust to having a happy, energetic daughter—or will Mom insist that Susie be "just like Mommie?"

In studying mother-daughter relationships in literature, we were intrigued by Louisa May Alcott's book, *Little Women*. It is evident here that the characters Jo and Marmee quite closely resembled the true-life personalities of the author and her own mom. From Louisa's true-life story, modern-day mothers can certainly learn about encouraging their daughters. For, on Louisa's fourteenth birthday, her mother gave her a pen and told her daughter prophetically, "Believe me, you are capable of ranking among the best."

How can mothers encourage their daughters toward goodness, happiness and greatness? Can we learn from the characters in literature? Is it possible to raise daughters—infants, young children, teenagers and young adults—and *still remain friends*?

In order to answer these questions, let us now consider several different factors which highly influence the lives of mothers and daughters. And, for one who both has been a daughter and is a mother of a daughter—experiencing the excitement, pleasure and frustration of both roles—indeed, this writing truly "hits home."

Mothers and Daughters— Whose Life Is It Anyway?

1. *Your daughter's independence.* She is not a "little you"; she is her own person. Allow her the freedom to be herself; praise her accomplishments. Through love, kindness and patience, give her your help and support.

Marie Curie was one who believed in this philosophy. She vowed: "I don't want to interfere with my child's development for anything on earth." Indeed, her daughter, Irene, grew and learned and achieved, and both Marie Curie and her daughter Irene were awarded Nobel Prizes for work with radioactivity.

2. *Mom's independence.* A mother who has developed a strong grasp on her sense of self can offer her daughter an inspiring role model. Do you value your own achievements? Do you pursue your own special interests? Are you growing as an individual person?

A young mother gave us food for thought recently. She sighed, "I'm Bill's wife and Susie's Mommie, but my real name is Jane...and somehow I don't know who she is anymore."

3. *Conflicting standards.* This is an enormous issue. Are your moral standards firm and strong? Are you confused about giving advice to your daughter regarding "what is right and what is wrong?"

How do we search for solutions to this dilemma? Frequently, our moral codes are shaken at their very roots. And many times, when life becomes confusing, mixed up and overpowering, the very best solution is to turn to God in honest prayer. Ask Him to help solve the problem; let Him share the worry, and place trust in His ability to see you through.

4. *Only one way...mom's way.* A teenage girl wrote in her diary one night, "My Mom and I will continue to fight forever and ever.... You see, there is only one correct way to do anything ...her way."

5. *Vicarious living.* Many mothers do not set their daughters free. Long ago they abandoned their own dreams, as their mothers did before them, and now they expect their daughters to fulfill all their lost ambitions. Vicarious living is frequently disappointing.

Being aware of certain difficulties and problems in a mother-daughter relationship is generally stepping at least half-way toward the solution to the problem. We hope that this chapter will help to increase awareness for the reader (and the writer!) and hopefully, we will all remember the power of love and trust and gentle guidance as we raise and nurture our precious, wonderful gift from God—"a girl for me!"

9

Is Your Child Spoiled?

The "spoiled child" is a disappointment to the family, to society-at-large and to the child himself.

Spoiled children are like poorly-tuned violins; they annoy us, strain our patience and cause our heads to pound and ache. They cry, they scream, they pout and mope...they are unhappy, lonely and frustrated. Boys and girls who are labeled "spoiled" can be found in large families, small families and also among the rich, the middle class and the poor.

What should we look for when considering the whole idea of "to spoil or not to spoil"? First, let us consider twelve factors which are frequently present when children become spoiled. Then, we will investigate ways to help these children.

Is Your Child Spoiled?

1. Does he frequently exhibit poor behavior, disobey the family rules or use unacceptable language?

2. Does she frequently ask for *more* toys, *more* clothes, more, more, more of everything? Do you always buy her everything she wants?

3. Does he always get his own way? Do you dare to say, "No!"?

4. Does she help with chores around the house? Do you expect that chores be done well and completed on time?

5. When something wrong happens, does your child always blame it on someone else? Can he say, "I'm sorry"?

6. Does she have a selfish approach to life? Does she have a "give me, give me, give me" attitude?

7. Does he feel that friends always come first and family always comes second?

8. Is your child disrespectful in the manner in which she talks about parents, teachers, clergy, sisters, brothers and your adult friends? Does she forget to say "thank you"?

9. Does he study only the subjects which interest him?

10. Does she frequently make fun of others? Is she a master of "the put-down"?

11. Does he believe in the following philosophy: "If it's difficult or unpleasant, don't do it!"?

12. Is she constantly whining, complaining or crying?

Children who exhibit spoiled behavior are not happy boys and girls. Therefore, parents who decide not to spoil, but instead set limits, boundaries, rules and values for their children are fostering feelings of security and well-being. These children realize that Mom and Dad truly care about their growth and development. Family love and concern for others flourishes in an environment which discourages the spoiling of children.

Indeed, we may all wish to be spoiled and pampered once in a while! (A cup of coffee in bed on Sunday morning, a surprise gift, or going out for lunch!) But the child who is allowed to grow up like a weed in the garden—with no careful cultivation of values—will most certainly become tangled and tormented in the world of the "turned-off" and "tuned-out."

The following suggestions have helped many mothers and fathers raise their children in an unspoiled manner. We hope they will help you and your children.

How To Raise
an Unspoiled Child

1. Set a good example. Our children are observing our lifestyles every day. The days of "Do what I say, not what I do" are gone forever.

2. Supply generous amounts of love, praise and attention each day. Words such as, "I love you, honey!" are needed and appreciated.

3. Consistency is extremely important. We cannot say "yes" today and "no" tomorrow. If the rule is: "No jumping on the couch," then this rule should apply every day.

4. When we establish family rules, we are letting children know the do's and don'ts of living. We must also enforce these rules.

5. Spanking, when used infrequently, is an acceptable means to aid in enforcing rules for the *very* young child. However, it should *never* be done in anger. For older children, spanking is considered by many educators and psychologists to be harmful. Use others means of punishment for older children. As soon as they can understand what you mean, refrain from spanking.

6. Punishment is sometimes necessary in order to enforce the rules. Some effective punishments include temporary loss of: television time, bike-riding time, allowances, the use of the family car, etc.

7. It's O.K. to say "no." "No" can mean: "I care about you," "I want to help you," and even, "I love you." Parents who dare to say "no" are courageous, because many times it really is easier to say "yes," and then to add, "Do what you want, just don't bother me!"

8. Mothers and fathers who enjoy various activities together with their children generally have fewer spoiled sons and daughters.

9. Teaching manners helps to unspoil. Saying "Thank you," "I'm sorry," and "Excuse me, please," is still in style. Writing thank-you notes, too, teaches children a sense of gratitude, appreciation of the thoughtfulness of others.

10. Parents who encourage conversations about a concern for other people (not just themselves) are fostering feelings of empathy and regard for others.

10

They Called Him
a Dreamer

They called him a dreamer. They said he was slow. He had already flunked four academic subjects this year; he had dropped out of Boy Scouts, and he had very few friends. He was labeled a failure...and he was only nine years old.

His Dad decided to "make a man" out of him and insisted that he join Little League Baseball. And so there he sat on the bench, shivering and biting his lower lip. He knew that the coach would not call on him—yes, he always struck out.

The score was 2-2, his teammates were jumping up and down in excitement. Maybe they would win today! However, he hardly noticed their yells and screams; his mind was far away from the baseball field. He was dreaming about butterflies with large black and gold wings; they were dancing in lazy circles, resting on velvet marigolds, and then flying toward the soft clouds in heaven.

He loved to dream about butterflies; they were his favorite fantasy. Sometimes the butterfly pictures would slip out of his mind and would be replaced by scenes of a full moon riding high in the sky above a purple and black ocean, or other times he would dream about a large rock embedded with a thousand sparkling diamonds of mica. In his own private universe, he listened to the voices of living things; he called this his "forest music": the croaking frogs, the calls of songbirds, and the whispering, laughing leaves. This was his world; these were his friends.

If Rachel Carson were still living today, she would not be harsh in her judgment of this young boy. Together, they would probably wander joyously, hand in hand, through meadows and forests and along mountain streams. Perhaps she was thinking about these sensitive children, who are often misunderstood by parents and teachers, when she wrote her last book, *The Sense of Wonder*. In it she spoke of those who dwell among the beauties and mysteries of the earth. She felt that they are never alone or weary of life.

Unfortunately, when children are forced to join sports teams, labeled as failures in school and ridiculed by family and friends because they do not fit into the "accepted" mold, they become discouraged, disillusioned and defeated. Their only crime is their "uniqueness." Some may call it "weakness," and others may scream "stupid," "dumb," or "reject!"

We urge you not to give up on these tender, impressionable boys and girls. They may have great difficulty with spelling, reading and math; they may never hit a home run or make a touchdown; they may never win a popularity contest or be a part of the "inner circle"—but their value, their worth, their identity is truly awaiting discovery.

The pages of history attest to the fact that the "weak" in our society are quite frequently those who bring about significant change. Since they do not fit in with the established patterns and norms, they create their own. It could have been the "weak" of our human species who made the first weapons and tools or invented the plow or the wheel.

Yes, the "weak" ones among us—the different ones—have inspired us throughout the centuries. When we read of the unique glories of Joan of Arc, John the Baptist, Thomas More, Francis of Assisi, Mother Teresa and Ignatius of Loyola, we realize that "to be different" often means "to triumph."

Yes, these nine-year-old dreamers, these lovers of beautiful butterflies, are often our future change agents. One day they may take the vanguard in economic, political, religious and cultural fields. Let us not snuff them out with criticism and rejection before they have hardly begun.

And in their growing-up years, it may be painful for them to stand alone. For nothing on earth is so poignantly sad as the individual who must stand alone. Such dreamers become fugitives (we may call them our fragile folk), and they rarely get their own way. But when they dare to persist, they can conquer seemingly insurmountable obstacles and eventually bring about momentous achievements.

When we read accounts of the first free men and women, the first adventurers and explorers, we quickly realize that these were the "different people," and that because of their uniqueness and their courage they became the seeds of Greece, of Rome and of America.

11

Guilt Is Like
a Black Crayon Mark

> "Love bade me welcome:
> Yet my soul drew back,
> Guilty of dust and sin."
> —George Herbert

Guilt is like a black crayon mark; heavy, overpowering, and hard to erase. When parents or children continually bear the brunt of guilty feelings, they can become anxious, ineffective, and incompetent.

Guilt is defined as an emotional state caused by a person's awareness that he (or she) has done, or is doing, something harmful to himself or others, something that he knows is disapproved, even though it may not be expressly forbidden by law.

We spoke to a young mother recently whose nine-year-old son had confided to her: "I stole candy from the supermarket." He had had many nightmares about this theft. She advised him to confess his mistake, ask for forgiveness, and look for happiness, not guilt.

It sounds so simple: confess, ask forgiveness, be happy. Yet, as we talk with parents about their problems in raising their sons and daughters, we become increasingly aware that the guilt often lives on. Parents feel guilty about their screaming and swearing; they feel guilty about their lack of discipline; and they feel guilty about their children's behavior.

In *Don Quixote,* Cervantes wrote, "Let us forget and forgive injuries." And it is here we must begin. If we do not forget and forgive, the claws of guilt will tear at our emotions, wounding our heart and soul. These wounds from prolonged guilty feelings often cause the following effects:

1. Feeling of anxiety.

2. Fear of rejection and criticism from others.

3. Diminishing self-esteem.

4. Ineffectiveness in work and in family and social relationships.

5. Inability to cope well with daily problems.

6. Inability to work well with others.

We listen to parents' stories about their children. We read of the upsets, the turmoil, and the disasters within family circles. Some children grow up and turn to drugs, to "living together" without marrying, to different religious beliefs, and to many other styles of behaving and living. Parents ask: "Where did we go wrong?" "Where did we fail?"

Many mothers and fathers are haunted by the failures of their children. They spend sleepless nights and anxious days wondering, worrying, and accumulating more and more guilt. Guilt, however, is not the answer. Guilt is not the way.

May it be said that at the end of the second millennium we, as parents, learned to turn our guilt into guidance. For, when guilt is turned into guidance, it is like going from darkness into sunshine. Guilt is full of tears and sorrow; guidance brings hope and love and caring.

It is never too late to offer guidance. For older children who have strayed away from our values and beliefs—we can offer them our friendship, our love, our caring, our hope, and our prayers. To slam the door on them because they have found a different way will never bring them home again. Love can move mountains; rejection will not even lift an anthill.

For younger children, parents have an excellent opportunity to guide and to teach because these children are still living at home. The following list has helped many parents lead their children toward proper behavior and high moral values:

1. Help them avoid those acts which cause guilt.

2. Don't condemn them for minor offenses (spilling a glass of milk, etc.)

3. Teach them the importance of their relationships with other people.

4. Teach them to avoid dishonesty, irresponsibility, disloyalty, illegal drugs, improper use of alcohol, and other undesirable behavior.

5. Teach them principles of acceptable and proper sex conduct.

6. Prevent guilt feelings by constantly being aware of the children's need of self-esteem and by giving the children continuing nurturance and affection.

7. Provide for the children through your own lives the best possible examples of acceptable behavior.

8. Inform them of proper observances of civil laws, ethical codes, religious beliefs and cultural customs.

12

Handling
Mid-Life Crisis

It was Monday morning; he stared at his reflection in the mirror. Feeling tired and discouraged, Jim tried to ignore his greying hair, slightly puffy eyes and wrinkled brow.

"Another Monday morning," he winced. He went through the motions of shaving, but he could muster little enthusiasm for his work day, his family or his life. Today was his forty-sixth birthday, and he did not have a positive picture of himself growing older.

"I'm middle-aged," he sighed. He thought in terms of loss and decline rather than of growth and development.

This issue is a personal problem for many parents. It may begin as early as age thirty, or as late as age fifty. Psychologists call it, "Mid-Life Crisis." Since mothers and fathers have few maps and charts to guide them through these years, there are some who trudge and stumble along, coping stoically, ignoring their unique needs and capacities.

This type of home environment affects children in a negative manner. There is little enthusiasm, hope and fun if mid-life crisis hits with a resounding blow. Therefore, it is important to recognize its symptoms and learn about ways to relieve this problem.

The following questions will help you to take stock:

1. Are you frequently bored, restless and discontented? Are you unhappy at home, at work or in leisure activities? (Marriages are particularly vulnerable to mid-life crisis. Divorce and changing partners may appear to be in style, but it is certainly not the cure-all for the unrest within your own personality.)

2. Do you hold on to hobbies and relationships that you have outgrown? ...The same old bridge game every Saturday night, the same circle of friends, the same vacation spot each year, the same route to work each day....

3. Do you feel negative, cynical, and without dreams, plans and enthusiasm for next week ...next month...next year?

4. Are you preoccupied with fears of death or illness?

5. Is insomnia, depression and illness a way of life for you?

6. Have your children, relatives and friends moved away from you, making you feel lonely and depressed?

If you answered yes to any of the previous questions, you are probably experiencing some form of mid-life crisis. Parents who recognize these symptoms should realize that they are not alone in their plight. Mid-life years have dealt a frightening blow to numerous mothers and fathers. Those who survive this period look upon their problem as a challenge. They see it as a time for creative work and major growth opportunities.

How do you begin to make some changes? Naturally, you want to feel better, look better and become happier. Therefore, let's begin with pen and paper and write down the major achievements in your life. Include here such events as: graduation dates, various jobs which you've held, marriage, birth of children, new interests, sports and hobbies, new friendships or exciting vacations. Try to keep this list up to date.

Next, write down your future goals. They may be: making a new friend, taking a course, writing, painting, repairing the car, looking for a new job, getting married or losing weight. When we write down our new goals and place the list on the bedroom bureau (or some other obvious place), then, we are more likely to work toward these new goals.

Make another list of people in your life who are truly important to you. Include them in your plans, enjoy their friendship...they will give you strength and hope through difficult times.

Think about what gives you your inner strength. This could be an excellent time for you to study philosophy, religion and related sources which give life its true meaning. Many parents have told us that when they decided "to return to God's love," their depression grew dimmer and their horizons shone brighter.

Recently, a mother in her forties told us her story. She had been depressed, lonely and fearful about growing older. Then, she had decided to stop worrying about herself and turn her energies toward concern for other people. Her days are filled now with small, kind acts in helping neighbors, friends and those with whom she works.

"I feel younger at forty-five than I did at thirty!" she exclaimed. "I don't have time for a mid-life crisis anymore; besides, it was so boring when all I thought about was myself!"

13

The Power of Touch

Do you remember how you felt when you were ten years old, with freckles on your face and skinny legs, and you believed that not a soul in the world loved you? It probably began when you bought a big ice cream cone at the neighborhood drugstore and relished the first two licks and then all the ice cream wiggled off the top and went splashing to the ground!

Or, was it the day you rode your bicycle to your friends' home and nobody would talk to you because you didn't fit in with this bubblegum-chewing crowd?

No matter how it began, you found yourself sitting on the front steps, tracing circles in the sand with a large stick and watching your teardrops turn the sand into mud.

And then your grandma came along and patted you on the shoulder. She offered the kind words of Grandma Wisdom, and all the time, she rubbed your shoulder and told you not to worry.

Ten minutes later, you felt much better; you had probably forgotten all of your grandma's advice, but her gentle, loving pat had warmed your heart and had given you courage to try again.

Yes, there is something about this "power of touch" which is a necessary part of parenting—and, indeed, also of "peopling!" (Is that a new word?) Our relationships with one another improve tremendously when we dare to reach out, to care—to touch.

Physicians are discovering more and more each year that when they touch their sick and dying patients, it soothes, it comforts and it also heals. To stroke a sick person's arm, to hold his hand, to pat his head—all of these can be more powerful than the strongest drug.

Those of us who are mothers and remember the pain of labor and childbirth can attest to the fact that a nurse's touch helps to ease the pain and speed the delivery process. A young mother wrote in her diary many years ago: "When my first child was born, I squeezed the nurse's hand so tightly that I thought I would injure her for life! But I needed to get strength from her. I never saw her again, but I'll never forget the courage she gave when she offered me her hand."

The power of touch—it has existed for a very long time. Hundreds of years ago, it was immortalized in the Sistine Chapel in Rome. Michelangelo must have highly valued this lovely act, for in the holy chapel you can look up and see his masterpiece. And you may become misty eyed as you gaze at this beautiful portrayal of God giving life to Adam through the touch of His hand.

As parents, what can we learn from all of this? How can we become more in tune with our feelings and not be afraid to share them with family and friends? When was the last time you cared enough to shake a hand or touch an arm or pat a shoulder?

Indeed, many of us are shy and awkward and not schooled in the gentle art of touching. Our society tells us, "If you touch, you will be considered aggressive—or worse still, overly emotional, or sexy."

Curiously, there frequently appears to be no happy medium in the touching world. Therefore, we keep our distance and play it safe. After all, who among us wants to be rejected or labeled foolish or become embarrassed by what others might say? Clearly, we are from pioneer stock; our ancestors braved the stormy Atlantic or Pacific and our heritage boasts of independence, courage and rugged individualism.

But, we are also feeling creatures, craving emotional nourishment from one another. And when we gather enough courage to reach out to our children, relatives and friends—be they one or twenty-one or fifty-one—then, we are showing our care and concern for others. We are becoming powerful communicators through these gentle, outward human acts. A handshake, a pat on the shoulder, a hug or a kiss (when appropriate)—all of these are important parts of parenting—and peopling, too!

14

Grandpa's Philosophy

A baby boy! Born today; soft and warm and shiny new; blue booties, sleeping, crying... loving.

"He has all the time in the world!" says Grandpa. Like a canvas with no painting, like a newspaper with no print, or like a music staff with no notes—this baby boy has an abundance of time—time to create the pictures, words and music in his life.

What advice would you give this baby boy, Grandpa? You have lived and laughed and loved; what wisdom can you pass along to this day-old infant?

He will not understand your words; he is too tiny; he is too young. But we will write down your Grandfather's philosophy, and perchance someday when he's twenty-two, he will read your creed, he will weigh your words, he will chart his course; and he will say: "Thanks, Grandpa, thank you very much."

Grandpa's Philosophy

1. *Take time to look and listen.* Look at people's faces; listen to their words. Whether you agree or disagree, look and listen, see and learn.

2. *Take time to work.* Work keeps us out of mischief, it keeps us productive, it makes us feel worthwhile, it enhances our self-esteem. Working pays the bills and keeps our country moving. Try to find work which is in tune with your personality; try to find work which you enjoy.

3. *Take time to play.* Sports, parties, friends, games, entertainment and fun! Playing is as American as turkey at Thanksgiving. Enjoy good food and drink...measuring cautiously, sipping slowly! Relax, unwind, take off your shoes and wiggle your toes. Be happy!

4. *Take time for your children.* They will soon grow up and like arrows from the bow, they will have a life of their own. Take time to talk and walk with your children; they are a most precious part of your life.

5. *Take time for old people.* Remember, they were once twenty-two. Talk to them, listen to them, learn from them. Older people are the strong foundation of our nation.

6. *Take time to read.* Books are the fountains of wisdom. Reading will keep you excited and enthused about people, places, ideas and things. Reading can open the doors to your dreams.

7. *Take time to enjoy nature.* The autumn leaves, the snow-topped mountains, the roaring sea...birds, flowers, grass and sandy beaches. These are pleasures which you will never have to sign on your mastercharge...they are free.

8. *Take time for your health.* We are given this precious commodity as a gift. However, most of us do not appreciate it until we have it no longer.

9. *Take time for love.* Love your spouse, love your family, love your friends. Love creates bonds of goodness and strength between people. It becomes our lifeblood, our salvation, our glory. Love enriches our lives. Let it grow in your heart; let it stir in your soul.

10. *Take time for God.* Your Creator...Your Master...Your Father in heaven. God is perfect Love. He is all-knowing, all-loving, and all-merciful. Pray for His help and guidance. *Place Him before all others;* honor His presence in your heart and soul.

15

Help for the Shy Child

15

Help for the Shy Child

Shyness, as a personality trait, has few references in quotable literature. In both novels and history, authors seem to prefer to write about bold, daring, courageous and adventurous characters; these individuals animate the lifeless pages and delight our minds and imaginations.

Hence, the timid souls in our world are frequently overlooked, pushed aside, and regarded as worthless. Like Caspar Milquetoast creatures, they suffer in silence, considering themselves to be second rate and incapable of merit, achievement and happiness.

Have you ever felt shy? Do you have a child who appears to be withdrawn, reticent and fearful?

The bashful child or adult lives in a world of anxious days and frightening nights. The bashful allow others to speak for them; they seldom question those in power; they swallow their unique and wondrous ideas, and they sit in silence—clapping, nodding, smiling and agreeing. Yet within their very being stirs all the apprehension and restlessness of a storm, and more than once they say to themselves: "Someday I'll speak up; someday I'll tell them how I *really* feel!"

However, day after day passes by. They are cute and doll-like in kindergarten, agreeable and "no-trouble" in grade school, and leave no mark of distinction as they graduate from high school. They never complain when an older brother or sister always answers the telephone and the door bell or greets a friend or neighbor at the store. When walking alone, they cross the street if they see someone they know approaching them. For it would be "horrible" to be forced to talk with Auntie Sue or Cousin Jane.

Shy children live in a semi-prison atmosphere. They are afraid to be themselves, and lacking in self-confidence, they rarely dare to try anything new or challenging.

Mothers and fathers ask questions about shy children and they wonder: "Will my child outgrow this personality trait?" Unfortunately, statistics reveal that shyness is generally not outgrown unless some effort is made to overcome the problem. In fact, recent studies reveal that 40% of our population is affected with shyness.

You may call it a maddening malaise, and wonder and worry about shyness in your children, in yourself or in an adult friend. We must realize that shy people—although often silent—truly do feel the sting when excluded from gatherings and keenly sense the non-acceptance of their associates, although they rarely speak of this. They somehow learn about the party, the game, the dinner, the good times...long after the others have gone home, long after the music has stopped playing.

With all the preceding information in mind and after observing each day various men, women and children, and after studying numerous books and articles, and after experiencing personal shyness from time to time, we offer the following suggestions to the introverts among us.

For the Shy and Semi-Shy

1. *Recognize your uniqueness.* God gave us all two ears and one mouth. Perhaps He had good reason for this; perhaps He wanted us to use listening twice as often as speaking. Therefore, if you prefer silence to talking, pride yourself in your ability to listen, learn, reflect and grow.

2. *The quiet members of our society* are often intuitive, thinking, imaginative people. Their artistic skills, their research ability, and their philosophical approach to life have produced remarkable achievements in music, writing, painting, invention and research. Therefore, if you are quiet, do not be shy in your approach to

life, but rather, value your skills and continue pursuing your special talents.

3. *Playing with hand puppets* can help a child overcome shyness. Let him or her speak through the puppet. Make a game of it. Act out an extemporaneous play; you hold one puppet and allow your child to hold another. Children are usually not bashful when performing in this manner.

4. *Encourage your child* to join groups, such as: church groups, scout troops, clubs, community activities, etc. Social groups help overcome shyness.

5. *Talk to your children.* Engage in daily conversations about exciting topics. Be enthusiastic. Talking is much more than giving directions and orders. Talking to a child includes a lively conversation about the interests of the child.

6. *Consider the "aloneness"* which exists in our world. Single parenting is lonely, divorce is lonely, being an only child can sometimes be lonely. Loneliness can cause shyness. Force yourself to seek the companionship, comfort and support of others. Remember each day: you are special and you are loved by God.

16

For Fathers—
On Fathers' Day

On the third Sunday of June, we celebrate Fathers' Day. And as families celebrate this special day, it reminds us of the Song of Solomon:

"For, lo, the winter is past
The rain is over and gone
The flowers appear on the earth,
The time of the singing of birds is come
And the voice of the turtle
Is heard in our land."

What "voice" do dads have in families today? Do we listen, as we should, to the ideas, words, conversation and advice which fathers give to their families? Is the American father appreciated, respected, honored and loved?

American fathers do not have an easy job. There are many forces, both internal and external, which complicate and confuse the role of fathering. The stress of work, the atmosphere at home, the high rate of inflation and the constant influence of negative daily news often disillusion and defeat many fathers. They feel they are not successful. Some call it "marking time"; others say they are "overwhelmed."

Perhaps fathers should take another look at this word "Success." Does success mean steak for dinner every night, a new car in the driveway, becoming president of your company, three beautiful children, and vacations in Europe each summer? Is success "never making a mistake," always putting your socks in the laundry and never yelling at your kids?... We feel that true success need not be any of these.

Therefore, what is successful fathering? We would like to answer this question by quoting the words on our office-wall plaque entitled: "What Is Success?"

> "That man is a success
> Who has lived well,
> Laughed often and loved much...."

To appreciate each day with its share of ups and downs, to laugh and to love—this is success. We think of bike rides along city pathways, ball games in backyards and laughter which echoes through hallways. Successful fathers love their children; they are accepting, forgiving and trusting.

> "That man is a success
> Who has gained the respect
> Of intelligent men and the love of
>   children...."

We gain respect when we listen and learn from those who are knowledgeable. Intelligent men are found in universities, on farms, in country stores, in factories and on city sidewalks. Some are truly fragile folk, but their philosophy of life is in tune with all the music of the universe. Successful fathers make time to talk with these intelligent men, women and children. Listening, learning and growing are essential to fatherhood.

> "That man is a success
> Who has filled his niche
> And accomplished his task,
> Who leaves the world better
> Than he found it...."

What is your "niche"? Is it possible to leave the world better than we found it? It certainly is. It is happening every day. Scout leaders, lay ministers, political leaders, teachers, counselors, volunteer workers, doctors, lawyers, musicians and many others are doing this. Some dads mend fences, some write poems, and some give swimming lessons. All are important; all are successful.

> "That man is a success
> Who looked for the best in others
> And gave the best he had."

In a 1948 yearbook from Johnson High School, North Andover, MA, we discovered an essay entitled "Success" by Mary Clare Milan. Although decades have passed since her graduation day, her thoughts remain highly significant. She wrote that successful fathers (and mothers) are often those who play a humble role:

"Those who are not averse to play with gusto a humble part are the most successful of all.... There are the mother and father who scrimp and save to give their children what they would like them to have. Who dream dreams not for themselves but for their offspring—who, they hope, will accomplish what they themselves were not able to do. This mother and father will not go down in history, but their sacrifices will be engraved forever in the hearts of their children, who alone will pay tribute to their memory."

Fathers' Day, Success, Happiness and Love. Each father and each family respond to these words in their own way. To live well, to laugh often, to gain respect, to fill one's niche and to give one's best are basic, simple truths of life. And when fathers combine all this with a trust and love for our Lord, they will most certainly have a happy Fathers' Day.

17

For Mothers—
On Mothers' Day

Mom. Mother. Mommie. Mum. She has many titles; she has many roles. And Mothers' Day is her day to be recognized, honored and loved.

How does a mother, who also tries to be a writer, find words to describe Mothers' Day? Indeed, one feels much too close to the scene; it becomes like looking into the mirror and remembering the prayer, "Not me, Lord, please call on someone else."

However, Mothers' Day is a beautiful, lovely day in May. It is a day for dinners and flowers, smiles and maybe a few tears, a time for hugs and kisses. You probably are thinking about your own mother, your grandma, too, and now you are a mother yourself. It all happens so quickly.

Mothers' Day gives us an opportunity to reflect upon all these generations of mothers. Yes, today let us consider "the stuff" of which moms are made. Complex. Complicated. Funny.

Loving. Serious. Sometimes angry. Sometimes frustrated. Friendly. Understanding.

If you are a mom, what words could we use to tell about you? Let's mix these words up, as if we were baking a chocolate cake, and see what flavors, tastes, memories and stories we can find. For there must be at least six different ways to describe mothers on Mothers' Day.

1. *Mothers are forgiving*. They forgive you for stealing candy, tearing your jeans, losing your pennies and breaking the window. When you are older, they forgive you for listening to loud music, coming home late, or losing your keys. (Maybe not right away, but eventually.)

2. *Mothers are human*. They can become discouraged, sad, lonely, frightened, overwhelmed and angry. They may lose their job and their best friend—all on the same day. The dinner burns, the dog runs away, the washing machine breaks down, and the price of gasoline skyrockets. And sometimes, they can be heard screaming, "......!" Yes, moms are human, too.

3. *Mothers are accepting*. When you gain twenty pounds, start to go bald, lose your front teeth, and spend your last dime, Mom still accepts you and says, "Tell me about it, Dear; it's all right, I understand." Very often their sense of humor comes forth at this time, and before you know it, they help you to smile and laugh at yourself, and you are ready to begin again.

4. *Mothers are loving*. They love their husbands, their children and their friends. To show their love, they bake cookies, drive car pools, volunteer their services and talents, teach religion classes, write letters and cards, clean the house, wash and fold the laundry, and buy food each week at the supermarket. And when they finish all that, they will stay up with you all night because your temperature reads 102°. Yes, moms are loving people.

5. *Mothers are understanding*. They understand how happy you can be when you get a new car, or meet a new friend, or go to a great party, or decide to get married. They understand when things go right and when things go wrong. They have a Mother's intuition which sometimes knows you better than you know yourself. And sometimes you think, "I hope she can't *really* read my mind!"

Mothers understand their sons' and daughters' needs and wishes. They guide their children as they look ahead toward the future. Some may choose a life in the religious world and Mom may hear one day: "I want to be a priest." ...Or "I want to be a sister." ...Or "I want to be a brother." The loving, understanding and accepting moms of our world are often the ones who encourage and support religious vocations for their children.

6. *Mothers are people, too*. Mom was once a young girl, then a young lady, a bride, a mother,

and perhaps now even a grandmother. She spends much of her time thinking and working for others, but she is a person, too. She requires understanding, love and praise from her family and friends. When someone says to her: "I like you," or "Thank you," or "I'm sorry," or "You did a great job!"...then, she shines, she glows, and she wants to do more. Kind words nourish mothers just as sunshine and water sustain plants.

Moms grow older, too. They slow down, get a few aches and pains, and sometimes become forgetful and difficult to understand. They may require hospitalization or nursing-home care. You may feel sad and lonely for them.

Their twilight years may sadden you, because every son or daughter certainly wishes the very best for his or her mother, especially on Mothers' Day. However, in the graceful, quiet solitude of old age, they rest and spend many hours sleeping, perhaps even praying. For now, in their own way, they are preparing for a new life, a new existence—the reward of eternal happiness.

18

Do You Have
Trouble Sleeping?

"O sleep! O gentle sleep!
Nature's soft nurse, how have I frightened
  thee,
That thou no more wilt weigh my eyelids
  down
And steep my senses in forgetfulness?"
        —*Henry IV*, William Shakespeare

She tossed and turned the night away, and although her weariness completely engulfed her, she could not relax, she could not sleep. The large white alarm clock on her bedside table read 1:00 a.m. She straightened her pillow, counted six hundred sheep jumping two by two over white picket fences, and relived all the details of yesterday, today and tomorrow. With a burning feeling in her eyes and a pounding headache, she checked the clock again. It was now 3:30 in the morning.

She had experimented with sleeping pills, aspirin, novels, alcohol, late T.V. shows and stargazing. She had complained to her doctor, yelled at her kids and daydreamed about running away to a Caribbean Island, where surrounded by lush palm trees, gentle breezes and a carefree climate, she would certainly drift easily into slumber each night.

It is called insomnia. This sleepless condition has caused numerous difficulties for mothers, fathers, and children in all walks of life. When we are refreshed with seven or eight hours of restful, comfortable, peaceful sleep, we solve our problems sensibly, we feel in control of our world, and we can smile and laugh at the humor or lack of humor in our world. However, when we are robbed of our sleep time our senses are dulled, our minds become fuzzy and our outlook is bleak and dismal. We long for a quiescent state of being; we pray for heavy eyelids, a relaxed mind and maybe even a snore or two!

Among the numerous causes of insomnia, *stress* is certainly a prime issue for consideration. Any event in our lives which evokes strong physical, intellectual or emotional demands can be draining and it can trigger the need within us for more sleep. Unfortunately, however, the very same event can also create a reduced ability to fall asleep.

The following list of "Don'ts and Do's" has helped many parents (especially mothers) regain their ability to sleep well.

The "Don'ts"

1. Stay away from coffee, tea, chocolate and cola in the evening. Any substance with high caffeine content can cause sleeplessness.

2. Stirring novels, controversial news stories and violent television shows do not produce a tranquil state of mind.

3. Those who drink excessive amounts of alcohol often experience many awakenings during the night.

4. Excessive exercise can cause insomnia.

5. Avoid naps during the daytime.

6. Going to bed early does not help.

7. Tight, binding clothes decrease circulation and inhibit sleep.

8. Bright lights, overly warm bedrooms, and noise all add to a non-restful state.

9. Do not use your bedroom as a work room. Bedrooms are for peace, quiet, solitude, loving and sleep.

10. Don't tackle family problems at bedtime. Learn to say, "We'll deal with this in the morning."

"Do's"

1. Develop rituals, such as: a relaxing bath or shower, brushing your teeth, applying night creams, etc. The soothing, comforting rituals before bedtime give our minds a subliminal message that everything is in order, all is well; and in spite of some turmoil, all is basically right with the world.

2. Try drinking a glass of warm milk (nature's sleep potion) before bedtime. Milk contains L-tryptophan, a substance believed to induce sleep.

3. If sleeplessness occurs, leave your bed and actually *write down* all the things you are thinking about. *Writing tends to make things real.* Read your written thoughts and say to yourself, "Tomorrow I will deal with these, one at a time." When we make lists of our problems, we bring order out of chaos and life becomes manageable.

4. Make certain that you are not worrying about security. Buy and install sufficient locks and try to feel safe and secure.

5. Say your prayers and read the Bible or some religious or inspirational book before retiring.

6. Count your blessings. Recount in your mind all the great and wonderful events of your life. We have all had our share of achievements,

happiness and good luck. Focus on the positive, and throw the negative out of your mind.

7. Think back to a pleasant event in your childhood—or visualize your last vacation. Pretend you are there again. Enjoy the beauty and splendor of it all.

If you have finished reading this chapter in the evening, we wish you a most relaxing, well-deserved good night's sleep. Try stretching, yawning and perhaps a little dreaming about life and love and happiness; close your eyes, and drift into a peaceful, restful state.

19

Is Silence Helpful
in Family Life?

> "A time to rend,
> And a time to sew;
> A time to keep silence
> And a time to speak."
>
> —Ecclesiastes 3:7

Silence is peaceful, silence is threatening; silence is loving, silence is spiteful. In 700 B.C. Homer wrote about this perplexing subject: "There is a time for many words, and there is also a time for sleep (or silence)."

We would like to explore the sounds and reverberations of silence with you today, particularly the waves of silence which roar upon your family shores when your children become teenagers.

"She was an enthusiastic, energetic, happy little girl," a mother recently reported, "and then she turned fourteen, and she became stubborn, silent and moody."

A middle-aged father discussed his situation with his boss. "My son and I had a great relationship for fourteen years. We went to ballgames together, we went shopping together, and we talked a lot. Now he is fifteen and I can't get through to him. He clams up, and he won't talk."

Psychologists, psychiatrists and medical doctors tell us that when boys and girls grow into the teenage years—especially ages thirteen, fourteen and fifteen—they are experiencing within themselves emotional, physical, social and intellectual development. Frequently, their body chemistry and personality are undergoing rapid changes and these youngsters often appear to be on an emotional roller coaster.

When parents ask them questions, many times these teenagers become silent or answer with brief, sarcastic or angry words. Young people feel that they are often "in crisis," searching, confused, doubt-ridden and fearful. They worry about their weight, dating or not dating, family relationships, friends, part-time jobs, school grades, and acne.

Furthermore, the family values which teenagers learn at home—what is right, and what is wrong—are constantly being challenged by their friends and peer-group pressure. A fifteen-year-old girl put it this way: "I always have to decide between doing something I don't believe in, or making my friends unhappy."

Parents find themselves in the middle of this confusion and controversy, and many choose "silence" at home as a way to cope. Silence means: "I don't hear you when you come in late at night."... "I don't see you when you drive carelessly."... "I don't talk to you about 'do's and don'ts" ...and also, "I will play the 'waiting game' until you are twenty, and then I will talk with you."

Silence is an easy route; silence can be golden. However, when teenagers and parents retreat into the silent game, they become aware of more problems, more hidden turmoil and more disunity within the home environment.

What can be done to achieve open communications at home? Is it possible to talk with teenagers when they are troubled by "growing pains"? A good friend told us a few years ago, "We need the *most love* when we are the least lovable." And this statement appears to be especially true for youngsters in their early teens.

When teenagers show signs of uneasiness, unhappiness and disinterest, this is usually the signal that they are crying out for acceptance, comfort and love. Parenting then becomes truly "an art," not a science. It is a time for carefully-chosen words, thoughtful listening and consistency.

Let us consider "consistency" as a prime factor in guiding teenagers. Consistency requires: *rules* for growth and development, *teaching*, which means helping teenagers understand the rules; *discussion*, which involves talking about the rules (and, at times, being open to change a rule), and *strength,* which means enforcing the rules. Consistency is not an easy task in parenting; however, it is the very essence in removing unwanted silence from the home and developing open, honest communications.

Finally, silence does at times have its proper place within the family circle. We cannot constantly preach and teach and reach out. We must respect the privacy which youngsters sometimes require; they truly do have a need for independence. We must know "when to back off" and "when to talk."

Let your teenagers know that you want them to "keep working things out." Let them know that you understand and that you are there to listen and to talk whenever they need you.

A sixteen-year-old girl said it quite well: "I love my mom and dad and we talk over many things together...but sometimes I need time to myself...time to think, time to grow, and time to dream."

20

The Pain and Trauma of Divorce

How do children feel when parents divorce? How can separation and divorce be explained to young children, to youngsters in elementary and junior high school and high school?

Over 70% of divorced couples in this country have minor children, and the number of children involved in either divorce, separation or desertion is over 20,000,000. The statistics are almost too vast to assimilate accurately and to comprehend. Your neighbors, your associates at work, your friends, your relatives, perhaps even yourself—we all become a part of this web which spins larger with each passing year and gathers within its woven fabric the vulnerable children of our modern world.

There is a beautiful prayer of the Christophers which we think about when considering the tragedy and devastating consequences of divorce, and it begins:

"Help me, Lord, to turn my pain
Into a gift which I can offer to others."

With those words as a model for consolation and hope, we begin to write—searching for ideas to offer understanding and insight to mothers and fathers who are raising their children alone.

Let us consider first the preschool child. Mommie and Daddy have recently divorced and this little boy or girl is aware of a definite change in the home atmosphere. Research studies have discovered that 80% of divorcing parents do not explain their new lifestyle to their preschool children. These parents become so caught up in their own problems that they do not take the time to sit down and explain the situation to their little ones. As a result these youngsters often become very confused, upset and bewildered. Sometimes their behavior regresses, and reports of bed-wetting, excessive crying, separation anxiety, temper tantrums and irritability are common.

Children ages two through six need a great deal of assurance at the time of divorce. They require extra amounts of love and caring. Psychologists tell us that they often feel that since:

"Mommie divorced Daddy,
then she may divorce me, too."

They frequently blame themselves for the separation and the break up. Self-blame and guilt on the part of the preschool child is quite prevalent. One little girl softly and sorrowfully cried through her tears, "I was a bad girl, I stole candy, I made my Daddy mad, and so they got divorced."

It therefore becomes extremely necessary to talk things over with the young child. One brave and wonderful mother told us how she handled the situation. She openly and honestly explained to her young son: "Daddy and I are not living with each other any more.... You see, Daddy and I fight a lot. It hasn't been pleasant. It is not good for us to be with each other. But we both love you very, very much. It was not your fault; it was our fault." Then she answered all his questions, and continued each day to love him and to trust him.

Children in elementary school also feel the pain and the distress when their parents' marriage fails. Members of this age group go through great anguish in trying to get their parents back together again. They are often persistent in their efforts for reconciliation; this many times is kept alive by one parent who encourages them in their endeavor. Elementary-school-age children frequently feel sad and abandoned at the time of divorce. Because of this, they have a strong need for sympathy and empathy. Support can be given to a child when the mother or father quietly and calmly consoles with words such as: "I know it is very tough for you not to have your Daddy (or Mommie) home.... I know you miss him (her) very much...but it wasn't good.... We feel it is better this way...but we both know how deeply it hurts you."

Grade-school boys and girls have tremendous longing for the absent mother or father. Some exhibit acute oppressive behavior and crying spells. Many will spend long periods of time alone in their bedrooms and when asked to talk about it will cry: "I can't talk about it." Children in this age group have tremendous amounts of anger—anger at their parents and anger at the world. They fight with their brothers and sisters, their peers at school and the parent who is raising them. When Dad visits, studies reveal that he can become a target of their anger, too.

When boys and girls in elementary school become involved in a variety of activities, they can become better able to cope with the divorce situation. School guidance counselors report that children who find interests at home and outside the home can deal more effectively with their world which appears to be falling apart. Sports, worthwhile friends, clubs, hobbies, music lessons, church and community activities are all positive opportunities for them to learn to adjust to their changing lifestyle.

When studying the effects of divorce on teenagers, we came across statements such as: "We stayed married until the children were teenagers, because we felt they could handle it then." However, the truth is that many teenagers are overwhelmed at this time with anger, sadness, great stress and anxiety. Some wish to keep the pain to themselves and not tell their friends and teachers. They feel a real stigma attached to their parents' divorce. The results of these feelings make it difficult for them to study and to concentrate in school, so that at times they lose as much as six months of school achievement.

Studies by school psychologists reveal that some mothers and fathers used their teenagers as supposedly useful tools, requesting them to carry angry and revengeful messages between divorcing parents. When questioned about this, these teenagers said they resented this role very much. As guidelines for parents here, we suggest: be civilized with your former spouse and do not use or unload on your son or daughter. They are not emotionally mature enough to handle a parent's distress at this time in their lives. Try to be open, caring, trusting, loving and understanding with your teenager.

What more can we say? There are volumes left unwritten here. We live in extremely difficult times. However, we hope we have offered some understanding and sensitivity for children and parents struggling with the pain and trauma of divorce.

21

Turning Things Around for the Rocky Marriage

- Betty knew that her husband Tom was having an affair with another woman.
- Joe found out that his wife Mary had a crush on another man.
- Jim couldn't stand his wife's heavy drinking habits.
- Sally's husband has been out of work for months. They fight and argue all the time.

The names are fictitious, the facts are true. These marriages are truly "on the rocks," and we hope today that we can throw out a lifeline and offer hope to parents who are contemplating divorce.

We have spoken with many divorced couples—and many of them are our dear friends—and they tell us:

—if only I had been more patient and understanding
—if only I hadn't been so angry

—if only I had tried to see his or her point of view

—if only we had remembered the good times instead of concentrating on the negatives in our lives.

In most cases it is the wife who suffers the most after divorce. She is left to raise the children alone; she must worry about paying the bills, educating the children and, yes, even fixing the washing machine. Many husbands marry again, and know little about the years of loneliness and heartache.

However, our intent is not to take sides. We certainly realize that fault and goodness can reside with both the husband and the wife. Therefore, let us begin by asking you not to dwell upon the pitfalls and high divorce rate which surround us. Instead, we must realize that marriage is a process of life. And like any growing thing, marriage needs loving, tending, forgiving and forgetting in order to survive and thrive.

Ten "Do's" for Rocky Marriages

1. Do remember that you fell in love and married to share a lifetime. No one of us is perfect. We all make mistakes.

2. Do realize that open, honest communications are necessary in marriage. No one can read another's mind. We must voice our feelings and

concerns. We must be understanding, loving and, most difficult of all, forgiving.

3. Do think, and when problems arise count to ten or even a hundred before speaking and before making decisions.

4. Do make time to be alone with your spouse. Children are wonderful, and we love them, but every couple needs a date at least once a week. (Even if it is only a walk in the rain!)

5. Do give your partner freedom. Let him or her grow as an individual. Respect the rights of one another and trust one another.

6. Do be affectionate. Hugging, kissing and walking hand-in-hand are still very much in style, at any age!

7. Do understand that every couple has a certain number of arguments and fights.

8. Do remember that you were once sweet-hearts—and you can be that way again if you truly care.

9. Do seek help from counselors, clergy or good friends. When we receive advice from others, our burden grows lighter and we can think more clearly.

10. Do pray to God for help and guidance. He asked that we love one another, and when we reach out with forgiveness and love to a fallen spouse, we grow in our love for God Himself.

Have you spoken recently with any divorced men and women? Have you observed the expression on their faces? Have you asked them, "Would you do it again?" Have you talked with their children and listened to their stories?

Perhaps it is the throw-away aspect of our society which tempts us all. Without thinking, we toss away plastic containers, paper plates and aluminum cans. Copying machines produce for us a duplicate of anything in print. And, self-service gas stations, banking machines and credit cards give us immediate access to so many of our needs.

However, our divorced friends tell us that if you throw away a husband or a wife or if you try to duplicate one, it becomes quite difficult. They go on to say that modern science has yet to invent a self-service spouse-making machine. Nor has mastercharge invented a buy now, pay later plan for finding a new husband or wife!

Truly, this creature called spouse can infuriate you, anger you and sometimes leave you close to tears. But he can also be your very best friend. When he listens to your problems, shares your joys and sorrows, and offers a helping hand, then we learn to realize why marriage is blessed and has been made a sacrament.

And so, if you are contemplating divorce as the next step in your life, we hope you will read this chapter once again. Then say some prayers to God, asking for His help. Remember many rocky marriages have turned around, and yours can turn around, too!

22

Let Music
Be an Important Part
of Living

> "Music must take rank as the highest of the fine arts—as the one which, more than any other, ministers to human welfare."
>
> —Spencer

Irving Berlin suggested that we "Say It with Music" and William Shakespeare wrote: "If music be the food of love, play on.... Give me excess of it.... That strain again!"

Yes, in our parenting philosophy we certainly agree with these men of words and song. And, indeed, above all others, Longfellow said it best: "Music is the universal language of mankind."

Do your children ever sing? Are records, musical instruments, humming or just plain whistling an important part of your home environment? Do you sing when you wash the dishes or stir the stew?

Some say, "I don't feel like singing. Life is too grim." And others tell us, "I have a terrible voice, out of tune, I *never* sing." And then we hear, "Today's kids only want to play and to listen to seductive songs, punk rock and loud, LOUD disco music." And finally, some parents tell us: "I want to throw that stereo out the window!"

Before we attempt to search for appropriate responses to the previous statements, let us turn first to the whole idea of music itself. None of us can deny the fact that music has influenced our lives: the love songs, the church music, the marching songs and the lullabies. Like a golden harp on an angel's wing, music enters our lives and changes our moods. Congreve explained it this way:

"Music has charms
To soothe a savage beast
To soften rocks
Or bend a knotted oak."

Have you ever heard church bells pealing in the twilight hour? Do you feel goose bumps up and down your spine when little children, clothed in choir robes, sing the "Our Father" or "Amen"? Music comes to us in many ways: a show tune, music from your car radio, television symphonies or the sweet sound of a young soprano.

Therefore, as an important part of parenting, may we suggest that you add more music to your life and also the lives of your children. A young mother recently told us: "My kids were fighting. It was snowing and blowing outside, and then I turned the radio on. They were playing a march. My four-year-old began to smile and my six-year-old started to march. I did 'left-right, left-right' along with them, and the fight was soon forgotten!"

Another story from a patient dad: "My teenage son had little in common with his old dad. We hardly spoke to one another. Then, I started listening to some of his records with him.... Overall I grew to like the sound. Music brought us together again.... I took time to stop and listen, and I won my son back through music!"

May we state emphatically here that music should never be forced upon a person. For when music is unwillingly thrust upon a child, the love of music can quickly turn into the hatred for music. Parents have related their memories to us. They include: "You must practice piano two hours every day!" Or, remember this one: "No playing outside until you've memorized that song! And play it on key!"

To force a child to become a fine musician is as ridiculous as insisting upon sunshine every day. Instead, boys and girls grow in their appreciation and love for music only in a happy, loving environment. We have been told over and over again that parents who enjoy good music themselves generally have children who want to sing and to play instruments.

To quote an undergraduate thesis: "One realizes that music directly imitates the ebb and flow of feeling, states of mind, moral habits, as well as different varieties of human character. Of particular importance is the fact that music can closely imitate more highly ordered feelings, attitudes, and traits of character, that we, as listeners, generally take for granted. Given this mimetic ability, music molds and channels our feelings, with its synthesis of harmony and lyrics."

Yes, music is often a mirror of our lives. And now, rather cautiously, let us turn to the issue of teenage disco, punk rock and music which is offensive to some ears. Through their music, could these young people be voicing their frustration with an unbending, non-caring world? As some abuse drugs and lose themselves in the lyrics of punk music, could they be telling us that somehow, somewhere there is a need for better parenting, more listening, more caring, more accepting, more patience, and more love at home?

The debate could go on and on. Why does offensive music exist today? What happened to the carefully taught nursery rhyme of long ago? "With rings on her fingers and bells on her toes, she shall have music wherever she goes." And what *kind* of music will she sing, wherever she goes? Does she have the right to choose her own music and sing her own tune?

What kind of tune are you singing today? We hope it is a song of hope and joy and cheer. Even if you must try very hard to be happy, the influence of your happy tune will be highly significant upon the lives of your children. Perhaps we would all do well to remember the song of Snow White. To the seven dwarfs she often sang: "Whistle While You Work!"

And now, as you vacuum your rug or drive the car or make your bed, let music be an important part of it all. Maybe John Dryden was thinking of this, too, when he wrote:

"The trumpet shall be heard on high
The dead shall live, the living die,
And Music shall untune the sky!"

23

The Pain and Sting
of a Put-Down

Have you ever experienced the sting and pain of a put-down? Has another person—or a group of people—turned your smile into tears by means of biting, hurting words?

Today, we would like you to consider the put-downs which exist in our everyday world. Some call them the decay of manners and others say that they strengthen our character and toughen us for the real world. But, clearly, amid the controversy regarding their value, we find an array of negative emotions. Like hoofprints on the sandy shores, put-downs pound their way into our personalities, and with a painful twinge we try to toss them away and forget their imprint on our hearts and souls.

Curiously, the put-down is an emblem for many people among us. Their symbol of speech is forever negative, with no regard for fellow-feelings. To dislike and to criticize others is their pattern of performance. "I can't stand him!" ..."Isn't she dumb!"..."Don't invite them, they'll ruin the party!"...And it goes on and on.

As a result of these harsh, unkind words, there are a large number of parents and children today who continue to ache inside from the wounds of put-downs. At home they hear: "You're a lazy, no-good kid!"..."You're just like your Uncle Harry, and he never amounted to anything!"..."When are you going to shape up—you're such a mess!"

In the home, it can become the rule to nurture children with discouraging, injuring threats, swear words and falsehoods. And after being tormented and chastised, many a young one has run outside to seek freedom and consolation by kicking stones in the back yard. Indeed, contradictions and mixed messages are a part of each of our lives, and never have we received more damaging blows than in the case of the put-down.

Along with put-down situations at home, there are also those which exist in school. The hazards found in some parts of the pedantic world could chill the warmest heart and pale the healthiest cheek. Sarcasm and disapprobation, skillfully administered, are at times the vehicles for educating and instructing. "Your paper is always late!"..."When are you going to learn how to read that book!"..."When your sister was in grade three, she could read. What's the matter with you?"..."Stop stuttering, speak up, I can't hear you!"

If one insists upon the rhyme or reason for the continued use of put-downs, it lies here: *What was done to us, we return in kind.* In other words, we know no other way. And when our patience is waning, our frustration increasing and our kindness decreasing, we strike out—we hurt and we injure those we love. The core of the put-down is often our inability to bite our tongue and to think before we speak.

To appall you further, let us consider brothers, sisters and peers and their respective role in the put-down. This group frequently has an unnerving affinity for putting others down. When we inhabit the same house or classroom, we can easily annoy one another and become like rowboats, battered and tossed about in the crosscurrents of a stormy sea. "He won't talk to me!"..."She's too fat and ugly!"..."He's a retard." ..."You smell, and you're dumb, too!"..."You have an awfully big nose!"

These distorted messages—given to children by children—are a chronic source of discontent. They pave the way for lack of self-confidence, low self-esteem and personality disorders in adult life. The put-downs of the young to one another are indicators of the need for more love and guidance within the home.

Furthermore, put-downs have been found in our places of work, at social gatherings and also within the religious community. And, regrettably, what seems to compound this problem is the ubiquitous negative overload in our daily lives. To relocate our focus away from the omnipresent put-down and toward a positive attitude is not an easy accomplishment. Many of us are all too often under the sway of discouragement. We feel the wind of discontent rising within our homes, our work places and our social and religious communities.

Perhaps the worst put-down of all is the put-down-of-silence. ..."I will ignore you," "I will not communicate with you, I will not speak to you." ...Silence is a war game in which you become a non-person, you do not exist, you are overlooked, disregarded and not recognized. Silence is cruel, it hurts, it torments. It is a device used effectively in the non-caring, "I'll get even with you" world. Silence is analogous to slavery, and the victims of silence are caught in the chains of masters who have never understood the message of the Man from Galilee.

Indeed, put-downs rupture our relationships with others at every conceivable level. Let us all pray for a world which is free from put-downs. Let us work for this within our homes, our schools, our places of work and our parishes. And to accomplish this goal, each one of us must learn to say: "I really can't change others; this must begin with me."

24

And Now It Is Lent

And now it is Lent.
A time for thoughtful parenting,
A season for prayer,
An opportunity to talk to our Lord.

No time is uncomplicated or tidy,
No one of us is made of whole cloth.
Our lives are a checkered fabric of ups and
    downs.

Through follies and discrepancies
We need Your help, dear Lord,
With our daily loom of life.

A Parent's Prayer About Discipline

Dear Lord, teaching children about right and
wrong, good and evil, is a very difficult part of
parenting. I need Your help and strength and
guidance. At times, it frightens me when I realize
the depth and scope of my task. I must teach rules
and standards and good behavior. I must not be
afraid to say "no." I must not waver in my belief

in law and order and goodness. Please help me to discipline my children because I love them very much.

A Plea for Patience

Dear Lord, sometimes I feel as if I have no patience. I want to scream and yell. I try to be a good parent, but my goodness turns into frustration when I see poor behavior, messy bedrooms and teenage disrespect. Please help me to understand my children and to be patient with them.

Please Help Me To Be a Good Role Model

Dear Lord, I know my children are watching me. They listen to my speech, they watch my daily activities and they seem to understand my thoughts. Please help me to be a good person, and then I can be a good parent. I must not be overly critical, negative, or judgmental. I must try to be hopeful and positive in all I think and say and do. This is not easy, Lord. Please help me.

A Prayer for Children To Be Themselves

Dear Lord, I understand that my children have lives of their own. They are not "little me's." Just as I am different from my parents, they must have the freedom to develop their own identities.

When they are older, if their beliefs differ from mine, I must not stop loving them. I must learn to accept and to love the uniqueness in each of my children. They will pave their own pathway in life; and I must always remain their loving parent, even when we do not travel the same road.

Please Give Me: Forgiveness

Dear Lord, younger children and older sons and daughters may sometimes disobey. When they are little, they may steal a cookie. When they are older, they may steal or cheat or become intoxicated. Just as Jesus forgave sinners when He walked among us, please help me to forgive and to forget the sins of my children. I know that it is only when we learn true forgiveness that we can call ourselves "Followers of Christ."

Thoughts About: Parents Are People, Too

Dear Lord, please help me to realize that I am an important person, too. I love my children and my spouse, but I must also consider my own emotional, intellectual, social and spiritual development. Help me to set new and challenging goals for myself. I certainly understand that my own personal attitudes toward life and living are of high value. Give me strength to grow in self-confidence and self-esteem.

A Prayer for Love

Dear Lord, Your Son was born in Bethlehem to teach us how to love one another. I need to learn how to love and how to show my love. I must not be embarrassed to say, "I love you." But this is not easy for me, Lord, because I was raised in a very different environment.

I must try to reach out: to touch, to shake hands, to smile, to hug, and to kiss. My children—at all ages—need outward signs of love and affection for their emotional nourishment.

And they also need my spoken and written words of love. For when I say, "I love you," I am giving my heart and soul to those who are near and dear to me. Teach me, Lord, how to love.

25

Volunteer Your Time and Talents

Have you or your children ever volunteered your time for an individual or an organization? Is volunteerism still in style today? When one offers time, talent and work for "no pay," is it "the right thing" to do?

As parents, we must all teach our children about the ways of the world. We attempt to tell them about good and evil, values and ideals, rights and privileges. And to this list, let us also consider the concept of volunteerism—that is, working for an hour, an evening, or even many hours during the week for no remuneration.

There are those among us who will say: "If you're not paid for your work, it is of no value."..."Volunteers are not appreciated, they get in the way, they slow down progress!" ..."People who work for no money are taking jobs away from those who really need work!"... And the list of comments could go on and on.

How do you react to the previous statements? Do you think that people should *always* place a price tag on their work? Do you discuss these ideas with your sons and daughters?

Our country today is going through an extremely difficult economic period. Many people are either unemployed or underemployed. Prices, costs, budgets, profits and losses are reflecting the strain of it all. A weekly trip to the supermarket will certainly verify these statements. We are living in rather frightening times. And you may question: "What does all this have to do with volunteerism?"

In attempting to answer some of these questions and comments, let us take a walk back through the pages of American history. We have all read stories about the explorers, the early pioneers and settlers, and those who opened up our western frontier. Times were not easy for these folks either. Survival was the name of the game.

When barns burned down, neighbor helped neighbor, and a new barn was built again. When crops failed, farmers shared with one another. When parents died of dreaded disease, children were welcomed into new families with love and care.

During war and peace, sickness and health, depression and prosperity, Americans have given freely and happily to one another. This is what has made our country strong and proud and wonderful. Often, we have ignored prices, costs, bills and wages. Our desire to help one another has given us a proud and beautiful heritage.

Adults have aided adults. And children who grew up in this type of environment have continued the proud and admirable practice of volunteering to help others.

Today is certainly a far cry from that period of early American history. However, for many the name of the game is still "survival." And volunteers are needed now more than ever before.

Volunteers are needed in hospitals, libraries, schools, families, churches, neighborhoods, day-care centers, nursing homes, parishes, civic work, fund raising, safety programs, and oral and written communications; the list is endless! Yes, in spite of negative comments and sighs of discontent, your volunteer efforts are appreciated and welcomed. Be proud that you can help at a time when our communities are desperately crying out for assistance.

If you or your children are volunteers, you are representing the best of everything that is American. You are a part of a long line of citizens who truly care about their neighbor and their country.

And how do you handle questions about rewards, pay, and incentives? Some folks may raise their eyebrows, half-frown and half-smile, and say "You do all that *for nothing?*" How do you answer? What do you say?

Perhaps at this time you remember that teacher who helped you for hours on end until you "really learned" your math fractions. Or maybe you remember your Girl Scout leader, who marched in every parade with you, and then bought you coke and cookies afterwards. Or do you remember the lady in your neighborhood who cooked supper for you the day your dad died?

And now it's your turn to help, to reach out, to give back to society what has been given to you. Your teacher has retired, your Scout leader has passed away, and your neighbor no longer lives on your street. But others are there, others need help.... What will be your pay? It may be a smile, a handshake or a kiss—the most valuable commodities which exist today.

26

Talk to Your Teenagers About Responsible Driving

Do you remember the day you passed your driver's test? Your eyes sparkled, your heart pounded, your smile broadened and you exclaimed: "Now I have wheels!...Freedom!...I'm grown up!" If you were really lucky, you drove the family car. Errands, trips, dates, or just riding around town—having your driver's license was even better than getting all A's on your report card!

The years slipped by. Now you are a parent, or maybe even a grandparent. Perhaps driving has lost some of the magic; it is routine, a means to get from one place to another; at times, even a chore.

But the exhilarating thrill of earning one's driver's license lives on for teenage drivers. For better or for worse, our young people yearn for their "wheels," "freedom," and "excitement," just as we did.

As a parent today, do you feel anxious about allowing your son or daughter to drive the family car? When you read the newspapers, listen to the radio or watch television, do you fear the dangers involved in teenage driving? We all know the stories so well. The horror, the grief, the sadness, the tragedies. Should we entrust the keys of the family car to those we love the most in the whole world?

Many mothers and fathers truly wish to answer the preceding question with a resounding "No!" They fear the dreaded accidents, the death reports, the danger of the expressways.

Having been raised on farmlands, in North Andover, Massachusetts, it would be quite easy for us to suggest at this time that we all return to the more quiet life of horse and buggy. Demolish the cars—no more gasoline bills, car repair charges, insurance bills or excise tax! (Unrealistic? Ridiculous? Yes, it's true. This cannot be our solution.)

Therefore, back to the world of today, back to the issue of teenage driving. Above all, impress upon your newly licensed son or daughter that a proper attitude is the most important part of safe driving—that is, eagerness to obey traffic laws and also willingness to share the highways with others.

Responsible Driving

Let us now consider four topics suitable for discussions between parents and teenagers.

Speeding. Speed kills. Therefore, drive according to posted speed limits; always drive at a safe speed. Reduce speed at night, in bad weather, or in heavy traffic.

Drinking. Drinking alcohol is a major cause of driving accidents. Warn your teenagers about the dangers of driving after excessive drinking.

Dangerous roads. Drive with extra caution on expressways, at intersections, on narrow country roads, on hills, at blind driveways, and on one-way streets.

Faulty cars. Do not assume that your engine, brakes, lights and steering system are always operating properly. All equipment should be tested frequently. The use of seat belts can reduce injuries or prevent fatalities in accidents. Remember also to check your doors, hood, hub caps, mirrors, tires and windows.

As a nation of people on the move, our romance with the automobile continues from one generation to the next. As parents, we all have an extremely important task; we must discuss within our homes the importance of "driving safely." Let us pray for safe driving habits for all.

27

Getting Children To Help Around the House

Did you ever wish to be a fly on the wall and quietly observe the way another family lives? Did you ever fancy yourself as Sherlock Holmes, Nancy Drew or Agatha Christie, investigating the problems of family life? Today, we invite you to join us as we attempt to solve a mysterious, age-old family problem. What is it? Are you interested? Our topic is "Getting children to do chores around the house."

The sun is beginning to rise as we tip-toe into the home of the fictitious Smith family. Aided by the use of a newly-perfected invisible spray, we are thankful that we cannot be seen or heard. Young Tommy, age seven, has been up for two hours. We follow his happy trail of sugared cereal kernels, orange juice spills and dirty socks. And then we see him in his bedroom, peering through a muddied bowl, staring at his goldfish. We trip over several piles of books, toys, school papers and a few non-matching mittens.

Suddenly, the scene changes. Mom is at the bedroom door, "Tommy, clean up this mess! Hurry up! And I really mean it this time!"

The sound of a hair dryer sends us down the corridor to Susie's room. We notice that Susie is a collector of records, boyfriends' pictures, magazines and opened (sometimes spilling) bottles of perfumes, shampoos and make-up. Her wastepaper basket reveals a flurry of torn-up homework papers. Some have found their target, others have not. It first appears that Susie has no clothes in her closet (poor girl!) but upon further investigation, we discover that they are all on her chair, and "Tiger," her cat, is sleeping atop this expensive, cloth mountain!

Dad's voice echoes through the house. "Where's my new necktie?" We see him hurrying between kitchen, laundry room and bedrooms, wildly searching for his tie, with only five minutes to go before his commuter bus leaves for the city.

Before we mislead our readers, let us pause at this point in our mystery drama and state that a writer writes best after having "lived" through the experiences which are penned. Therefore, to have known clutter, disorganization and messed-up situations is to have become truly acquainted with life itself. Hence, in no way are we assuming a "holier than thou" attitude. At times, our dirty sock pile could win first prize in any laundry contest, anywhere in the world!

Let us now return to the Smith household. It is 10:00 a.m. The children have left for school, Dad and Mom are off to work, and the only sound we can hear is the quiet tick-tock of the living room clock. The cat yawns, stretches and sleeps on—a very lucky fellow! The goldfish appears to be choking in his dirty little bowl.

Since this is not an ordinary visit, we can certainly expect the unexpected today. And, sure enough, we find a large red button on the kitchen wall, and much to our amazement we find that by pressing the button, we can make the wall talk. This wall has recorded daily family conversations, disagreements and frustrations. So let's:

Press the Red Button
and
Listen to the Wall!

"I am the talking wall
I'm trying to stand very tall
But, I huff...I puff...I listen...I frown.
These people are sending me clear to the
  ground!
I'm frightened, I'm tired, I ache and I
  pain,
I'd like to wash them all down the drain!"

"Day after day, I hear...
'Empty the junk, don't be lazy!'
'Clean up your bedroom!'

'When are you going to clean up this mess?'

'Who threw the newspapers all over the living room?'

'Who spilled the milk?'

'Wash the dishes and stop complaining!'

'It's *not* my turn to feed the dog; I did it yesterday!'"

With a flick of our finger, we press the red button and "tune it all out!" Who needs this kind of grief! The tone of impatient voices, the frustration, the disagreeable atmosphere could make one want to run away and never come home again!

We hope that the following suggestions will help your youngsters "pitch in" at home!

1. *Planning.* Sit down with your children and make a list of "what" needs to be done. Post the list and assign chores. Rotate the chores each week.

2. *Rewards.* Rewards help to motivate. Either a small amount of money, verbal praise and/or a special privilege encourage the completion of chores.

3. *Keeping track.* Recording helps to get chores done. Keep a chart on the kitchen wall and encourage the children to check off their chores each day. (No check, no reward!)

4. *Teaching*. Do not assume that they know how to do their chores. Careful, patient, loving teaching is essential.

5. *A feeling of importance*. Children who have daily tasks to do feel good about themselves. Their self-confidence grows and they learn that they must work and contribute to their family life.

6. *Do not be a perfectionist*. Perfectionists have ruined many a day in family life. If the bed has a few wrinkles in it, try to remain calm...and *keep smiling!*

28

What Is Love?

...When I say "I love you," what do I mean, how do I feel...what is your reply?

Love is innocence, love is trust. Love is also patience, forgiveness, awareness, beauty, compassion, loyalty and tolerance.

Poets have written thousands of words, pouring forth their ideas in their attempt to answer the question, "What is love?" For parents, the message of Christ teaches us: to love God and to love one another. And, as mothers and fathers, each of us must learn the depth and profound meaning of the world of love in order to deal with spouses, children, relatives and friends.

Do you ever think about the word "love"? Indeed, it is the most beautiful word in our spoken and written language. And, today, we would like to explore the many facets of "love," and hopefully, enrich our minds and souls with its goodness and beauty.

Truly, it is so much easier to say, "I love you," than to say, "I ignore you," or "I hate you."

Love builds bonds of friendship between people; it bridges the channel between strangers and friends. Love can be chaste, yet true; love can be part of friendship, with admiration, affection and trust as the building blocks and supporting iron girders.

Let us examine now eight meanings of love and try to apply them to family and friends.

What Is Love?

Love means:

1. *I trust you.* I do not question your every thought, word or action. I trust your judgment. It may not always be the same as mine, but, nevertheless, I respect your opinions.

2. *I forgive you.* If you spend too much money or drink or eat or smoke too much, I do not hold this against you. I have my faults, too. I forgive you because I hope you will forgive me when I stumble and fall. Forgiveness tests the very core of true love; it is the most challenging part of our lives.

3. *I am aware of your feelings.* I know your likes and dislikes. Sometimes you may feel hurt or sad or lonely. Love means: "I am here to help you, to see you through. I care about you and I want you to be happy again."

4. *I am devoted to you*. Through outward signs of affection, I show my devotion to you. Here, I realize that I must educate and caution my children about the different kinds of love and the limits and boundaries of love. For, true love which lasts a lifetime should not be built on cheap thrills, pornography, materialistic values, or free and easy games of sex.

5. *I give you freedom*. Just as a bird needs freedom to fly and to live, I will not crush your wings in a jealous grasp. I will give you freedom to move about and grow...and because I will not enslave you, I know we will always be friends.

6. *I will try to be unselfish*. Selfish love cannot survive. True love is seeking the best for the one who is loved. Sometimes this means giving 100% of the effort involved and not winning every argument or discussion. It also means biting one's tongue and counting to ten (or one hundred!) before reacting to a frustrating situation.

Love and selfishness can never survive together. If I must always have my own way, then there is something seriously wrong. Unselfish love means helping with the chores of daily living: cleaning the dishes, washing the clothes, folding the socks, cutting the lawn, cleaning the garage, picking up the newspapers, paying the bills, emptying the ashtrays, and yes, even feeding the cat!

7. *I must be loyal.* When you don't win first prize, I still love you. When your team comes in last, you gain twenty pounds, you lose your job, and you spill your soup...I still love you!

8. *I believe in you.* I believe in your goodness. I accept you. I try to focus on your strengths (not your weaknesses). And when I tell you, "I love you," you seem to become stronger and happier.

Once, I thought that love was ephemeral, but now I have learned that love is eternal. Do you agree? What is your reply?

29

"I Must Set You Free"

"I love you, but I must let go.... I must allow you to be yourself.... I must set you free."

These are thoughts for parents of young adults. One of the most difficult roles of parenting is that of "letting go." Just as a baby cannot stay forever in the womb, your grown son or daughter needs to be given independence and wings to fly from your home nest.

How can mothers and fathers learn to let go? What should they do when grown children disobey? Should parents continue to love and to communicate with their sons and daughters when their values, actions and lifestyles directly violate family rules?

We will attempt to answer these heavy questions. And as we write, please realize that the words do not flow freely. For we have received numerous calls and letters regarding the issue of "older children and parents" and it becomes quite difficult to address questions which are the very core of family wars and friction. Indeed, our nation shakes and trembles in the throes of open hostility within many homes.

As children grow up, we must realize that:

1. *Peer influence* is a strong force. Friends tempt one another toward goodness and also toward evil. Do you know what kind of people your children have as friends?

2. *The parent's role* changes. When your son or daughter reaches age eighteen or twenty, your authoritarian role should be replaced by a new relationship with your child. You are now more of a peer than a parent; a friend, not a foe; a communicator, not a commander.

3. *Your guilt* (if you have any) must be pushed aside. Statements such as, "It's all my fault," or "I should have been more strict with him," or "I didn't love her enough," will get you nowhere. Guilt is negative; it is personally destructive.

4. *Your advice* is still important. Learning to be an older parent does not mean that you never speak, never advise or never communicate. Therefore: talk, discuss, reach out and share your opinions with your grown children. However, your main goal should be that of assuring your son or daughter of your continued love and commitment, realizing all the time that decision-making now rests with your offspring.

A forty-five-year-old father recently told us his parenting philosophy. He has raised four children and he explained: "I tried to develop independence in these youngsters all the way along. I knew that one day they'd be on their own, so I encouraged them to tie their own shoes, make their beds, hold down paper routes and learn to drive the car.... I knew that if I refused to give them appropriate freedom and independence, they would either rebel or become immature."

How Do Parents "Let Go"?

Remember that *patience*
Is here to stay.
It must be your watchword
Day by day.

Remember that *decisions*
Are no longer yours;
They are big boys and girls now
With their own chores.

Remember to *pray*
And ask for God's care;
Be loving and kind
Forgiving and fair.

Perhaps one of the most important roles of parenting the young adult is helping him or her choose the right job or line of work. If your son or daughter is happily employed, you should receive an A+ in parenthood! It makes "letting go" so much easier if your child has:

- Opportunity to learn a trade or profession
- A steady paycheck
- Career satisfaction and enjoyment.

Finally, we would like to point out a concern of ours. As we use words such as son, daughter, children, baby and offspring, we realize that part of the problem in "letting go" could be that of language. We have no word for "older children." Some of us may still be calling them "children" when they are twenty-five or thirty or forty!

Do you have any suggestions for a new word which would mean a grown child? Maybe if we had a name for these young adults, we would have fewer family problems.

30

A Closer Look at Drugs and Alcohol

Thirty years ago the word "grass" meant your lawn, "speed" referred to traveling fast, "trip" signified a vacation, "coke" stood for soda, and "hash" was your dinner on Thursday night. Today, however, these words and many other terms have acquired new meanings. If you talk with teenagers, young adults—and some older adults, too—you will find that these everyday words are the language of the drug culture.

Are you concerned about the ever-increasing use of marijuana, cocaine, alcohol, heroin and the multitude of other hallucinogens, depressants and stimulants? Do you worry that your young son or daughter might become a part of this no-longer-fringe society? Do you realize that many parents know that their kids smoke pot ...and vice versa?

In attempting to research, understand and write about the drug culture, one feels a certain sense of insecurity and also the weight of many unanswered questions. We have attended seminars, lectures and community events where we have learned about teenagers and their growing use and abuse of drugs. And when the talks were over and the lights turned out, we joined our friends for good food and drink.

We gazed about the gorgeous cocktail lounge and dining room and thought, "It's like being between trapezes," or what should we hold on to? Is it all right to sip fine wine and then say "no" to your students about drugs?

To add to the confusion here, we remember listening to a group of college students who were discussing the pros and cons of marijuana. One voice could be heard loudly and clearly above all the others:

"My Dad finishes his six pack and then screams at me because he found a joint in my room!"

How do we respond to these problems? Can a parent keep his or her perspective today and not be swayed by the crowd? Does peer pressure exist on both the teenage and adult levels? Where lies the truth?

As in many difficult situations, knowledge, facts and intelligent reasoning are generally the best route toward workable solutions. When we argue, employing only emotional reactions and outbursts, it usually gets us nowhere. Therefore, let's take a look at some of the facts about drugs.

Facts About Drugs:

1. *Marijuana* — (Source: Colombia and United States, Price: $40-$70 per ounce) The effect from this drug generally lasts from two to four hours. Although studies reveal that fewer people are now smoking marijuana, it still remains a popular way to "get high."

2. *Cocaine*—(Source: cocoa plants in Bolivia and Peru, Price: $100-$140 per gram) Cocaine is a drug which one sniffs. Its effect is about one or two hours and this drug is used mostly by some well-to-do executive types and affluent students.

3. *Alcohol*—(Source: legitimate distilleries, wineries and breweries) Heavy drinking of beer is a common scene on the college campus. Also, an "in" word about town is "polydrugs," that is, using more than one drug at a time. A Saturday night stroll through the campus scene will reveal students with a beer can in one hand and a joint in the other.

4. *Heroin*—(Source: Iran and Pakistan, Price: $250-$300 per gram) Rarely found in high schools or colleges, this drug, which users inject with a needle, is a narcotic of high physical and psychological dependence. Its effect lasts for three to six hours.

The Price Paid for "Getting High"

(For both young people and adults)

- *Achievement* in school is no longer a goal. Drugs become more important.
- *Memory* is adversely affected. Recent events and facts grow hazy in the mind.
- *Personalities* change. A once energetic, optimistic, fun-loving person sinks into listlessness and laziness.
- *Personal appearance* is downgraded. Fingernails, haircuts, clothing and baths are no longer important.
- *Family life.* Since the users experience feelings of guilt, loneliness and isolation, their relationship within the family turns hostile. Fighting and friction abound. The drugged person wishes to stay alone or remain with others like himself or herself.

What Can Parents Do?

1. *Explain* to your children the facts about drugs. Talk about the differences between legitimate drinks and illegal drugs. Discuss the meaning of "use" and "abuse" as applied to alcohol. Set a good example yourself. Seek professional help, if necessary.

2. *Encourage* your children's involvement in helping other people, in sports, music, clubs,

religious activities, school achievement and individual interests. When we "get high on life," we sniff the fresh air of success. It is pure and invigorating!

3. *Remember* the wedding at Cana and the miracle performed so long ago. There was no prohibition of wine at the Cana feast, and for those who are of age and who can drink sensibly, alcohol can be a legitimate means to enhance a celebration.

4. *Enjoy* the closeness and love of family living. Join together in worship of God. The family that prays together will stay together. And, truly, this is the best "high" of all!

31

Have You Taught Your Children the Facts of Life?

Are you concerned that your teenage daughter might become pregnant? Do you worry about the rampant spread of venereal disease? Do you talk about sex education within your home?

Sometimes we subconsciously reason that if we don't talk about a subject or if we don't think about a problem, it will go away. However, in the case of sex education for children, even though we may blush and stutter at the whole idea, it is not about to go away. Boys and girls become curious about sex—and the differences between males and females—as early as nursery school age. And, therefore, successful parents begin answering their children's questions about sex in an honest, easy style as soon as children begin to talk and to communicate.

Preparation Is Necessary

1. Go to the library and read some books. Be sure you understand what you are talking

about before you begin. There are many "old wives' tales" which still exist. Children need facts, not fantasy.

2. Decide how, when, where—and how much—information you will discuss.

3. Ask your doctor or school nurse if they have any printed information for you to share with your children.

4. Think about your value system. Develop for your children some rules and guidelines for dating and going steady.

5. Try to set a good example yourself. If your moral values are high—and if you live by your code—you are truly well prepared to meet the challenge of sex education for your children.

Preparation is important. However, putting all this into action is vital. Unfortunately, you will encounter many obstacles along the way. Some may be frightening, others could be called awkward and a few will be amusing. Perhaps the key to it all is to try to be understanding, adaptable and patient. If we become stern and authoritative, children frequently turn to their peers for support. Indeed, the whole idea of proper sex education within the home is a perfect argument for *love and limits* for parents, for children and for their friends.

Let us think about a few examples now and try to apply some of this philosophy to today's children in today's world.

The Age of Innocence

Susie (age 5): "Jimmy says his Mommy is having a new baby. How do you get new babies?"

Mom: "They grow within their Mommy's womb. And when they are strong enough, they are born. Babies need a lot of love."

When children are young, it is important to answer their questions honestly. However, a five-year-old does not need a complete biological explanation, nor is he or she ready for one.

The Age of Romance

Susie (age 16): "I love Jerry so much! And he loves me, too! Look at the new necklace he gave me!"

Susie and Jerry walk to high school together each day. They date every Friday, Saturday and Sunday evening. With few other interests, they are involved in a "heavy romance."

Mom (worried about the daughter because she spends many hours alone with Jerry): "That's a beautiful necklace, Susie. And your Dad and I are very fond of Jerry, too. He's a wonderful young man. But we are concerned about all the time that you two spend together, all alone."

Susie's Mom continues to explain to Susie in a non-threatening, loving style that there could be dangers in this kind of romance. She talks about one's emotions and the problems which frequently occur when two young people are hugging and kissing all the time. She suggests that Susie become interested in a larger circle of friends, and that she also join a basketball team, a photography club, the youth group at church, or another activity that interests her. Carefully and diplomatically, she talks about the frightening statistics regarding abortions, early marriages, and teenage pregnancies.

Susie may take her Mom's advice, or she may reject it. However, she has certainly been given wise and prudent counsel. Truly, she will not forget this conversation if it is accomplished in an empathetic, caring environment.

The Age of Discovery

Bill (age 17, talking with Joe, age 17): "Let's go over to Jane's house tonight. Her parents aren't home, and those two girls we met last weekend will be there."

(They exchange sly smiles and continue to talk about these girls, using language and gestures which are offensive and degrading to women.)

Dad (overhearing the conversation): "I didn't mean to eavesdrop, but I heard you guys talking. I know I seem as old as Moses himself, but let's talk about a few things."

Dad talks to the boys in his own style, trying to choose his words carefully. He explains to them that women are not sex objects; they were not put on this earth for men to exploit. He explains the dangers involved in promiscuity, one-night stands and sex without love and marriage. He talks about true happiness between a guy and a girl, happiness which is based on respect, shared interests and goals, and high moral values.

Teaching children our values regarding sex is probably one of the most difficult roles of parenting. We are faced with so many issues: our own anxieties and embarrassment, changing lifestyles, and the argument, "Everyone's doing it, so it's all right." However, if we do not overlook this important role in parenting, we are helping our sons and daughters more than words can say.

Your son may disobey you and your daughter might not listen, but nevertheless, you must persevere and keep talking, listening, communicating and most important of all, loving them.

And if your neighbors and friends tell you that you are "old-fashioned" and "too square," just wait a few years and let time tell its own story.

Indeed, some people are like bonfires with burning, racing flames, quick to ignite, blazing through the night, but scorched, burned out and destroyed by morning. Instead other people are like candles, with true, steady flames; their sheen and light and radiance touch all those around them; their glow never flickers. It lasts a life-time!

32

Baby-sitters
Are Important People!

"Baby-sitter" is an interesting concept. Taken quite literally, one pictures an older person sitting atop a bouncing, screaming baby. Or, maybe the baby himself is one who does nothing but sit all day. Indeed, words are fascinating vehicles for thoughts, but we must actually live within a certain culture to understand the true meaning of each phrase. Therefore, when we write "baby-sitter," we are sure you know exactly what we mean. Baby-sitters do not sit on babies —nor do they harm them in any other way— rather, a baby-sitter is a person who takes care of babies and young children.

As one who spent many hours as a baby-sitter during grammar school, high school, and college, this writer has viewed baby-sitting from many points of view. There were good children and also hard-to-manage children. There were screaming babies and laughing babies, and always, always those barking dogs. Memories still persist of lonely evenings in far-away farm houses, listening to the whistling wind and the scary noises of the night.

Time passed along, as it always does, and quite quickly we found ourselves looking for baby-sitters for our own children. Our best baby-sitters were Nana and Grandpa Murphy and Nana Hickey, too! If you are fortunate enough to have a grandparent for a baby-sitter, you are lucky indeed!

However, many young parents do not live near their families and it becomes necessary to find someone who is capable, trustworthy, empathetic and loving to take care of the children when Mom and Dad are not home.

Many parents have requested that we devise some guidelines for baby-sitting. Therefore, with this in mind, we offer you the following rules, first for parents and second for baby-sitters themselves.

Rules for Parents

1. *The interview.* If possible, interview several baby-sitters before selecting the best person. Ask for references and call these references to check on the baby-sitter's character and past performances.

2. *Your children.* Introduce your baby-sitter to your children. Nothing is more frightening for a young child than to awake in the middle of the

night and find a stranger in the house. Give the sitter and your children an opportunity to chat and get acquainted. Talk to your sitter about the likes and dislikes of your children and any special problems they may have.

3. *The tour*. Give the baby-sitter a tour of your home. The sitter should know your exits in case of emergencies or fire.

4. *Lock doors*. Make sure that all your doors are well locked. Check the locks before you leave and instruct your baby-sitter in the locking and unlocking of your doors.

5. *Telephone numbers*. Post on the wall, next to the telephone, all necessary telephone numbers. Show this list to your sitter. These should include the following numbers: your telephone away from home, the fire and police departments, a neighbor and a good friend or relative.

6. *Your rules*. Inform the baby-sitter of some of your rules. These could include the rules for: bedtime, television time, no running in the house, no fighting or yelling, no jumping on furniture, etc.

7. *Your values*. Discuss your value system with your baby-sitter. Use statements such as: "We expect the children to obey you and if they do not, please tell us when we come home."

8. *Books, games*. Provide a few books and games for both children and sitter to use together. This will help the time pass more

pleasantly and it will give both sitter and children a chance to enjoy one another's company.

9. *Snacks.* Children—and sitters, too—generally feel hunger pains from time to time. If possible, tell them about fruits, cookies, cereals or crackers which they may have when you are not home.

10. *A small gift.* Consider buying a small gift for your baby-sitter once or twice a year. We all thrive on love and kindness, and baby-sitters "sit best" for those who show their appreciation!

Rules for Baby-sitters

1. *Read* all the previously stated "Rules for Parents." Try to understand the importance of each rule and act accordingly.

2. *Realize* and value the fact that you are important. You are taking the place of Mom and Dad. Try to be as capable, trustworthy, empathetic and loving as possible.

3. *Remember* always that children are children. Do not expect them to be small adults.

4. *Think* about how you felt when you were a child. You probably loved people who would talk to you about your interests, people who would use your name in conversations, people who would listen to you, people who would play games with you or read books to you. And most of all, you most likely enjoyed people who would

say, "You're great!" or "You're wonderful!" or "That's a terrific idea!"

When you give children sincere praise, you are accomplishing one of the most important functions of baby-sitting. Truly, we all thrive on warmth, love and kind words from others.

In closing, we would like to offer a few thoughts for Mom and Dad. If your young son or daughter cries and makes you feel guilty upon the arrival of the baby-sitter, we caution you to remember the following truths:

• Many children cry when Mom or Dad leave the scene.
• Children usually stop crying within twenty minutes after your departure.
• It is good for children to become adjusted to other people in their lives.
• Children become more independent and self-reliant if they are not with Mom and Dad all the time.
• Baby-sitters are very important and very wonderful people. May God bless them all!

33

They Also
Deserve Forgiveness...

She sat on the large blue rug which covered her bedroom floor. With her knees pulled up to her chin and her arms encircling her legs, she resembled a china doll. Giant tears traced their way across her cheeks. She shivered and trembled. Although this child was only eight years old, she was experiencing once again the pain and anguish of an unhappy home.

Her mom and dad were in the kitchen screaming at one another. Little Betty pressed her chubby hands over her ears and cried.

"You've been out 'til midnight every night this week, Tom! I'm here with the children night after night, all alone, and I've had it!"

"What's the matter with you, Sue?" he shouted. "All you do is complain, complain, complain! I'm getting out of here!"

Then the door slammed as it had done many times before. Without thinking, Sue mechanically followed her well-trodden path into the living room, where the "medicine" cabinet was housed. She unlatched the scratched, old door and this unhappy mom poured a large dose of her adult liquid pacifier. It looked a lot like water, but it was labeled "gin."

We have called these story characters Betty, Tom and Sue. They could have other names, but their tale would be the same. Is there a family in your neighborhood, church, school or place of work that is undergoing similar problems? Perhaps you or some people in your family have felt depressed, isolated, unappreciated or unloved at some point in life. If this is true, we hope you will read on. For, we have spent many hours researching in libraries and talking with unhappy mothers about family hurts. And, in some small way, we hope that what we are writing here will help a family that is in pain.

Much of our research indicates that many mothers have low self-esteem. Their inner voice is always telling them:

● "I don't like myself."
● "I have few interests outside my home."
● "I am not even close to the man I love."

The results of these kinds of subconscious messages are feelings of being incapable, unworthy, not respected and not loved. Our self-esteem grows and flourishes when others appreciate us, communicate with us and praise us. However, if we are ignored, if we receive little attention or even insults from other people in our lives, then we are dragged down into a lonely valley of anxiety and depression. This hollow ground is frequently fertile with tears, arguments and alcoholism.

Let us take a closer look now at other issues which are willing catalysts in the area of family disintegration. Since we know of far too many "Sues" in our world, we will focus primarily on the plight of wives and mothers. A dear friend once told us, "If Mommy feels upset, the whole family feels upset, too!"

Why Do Mothers Become Discouraged?...

1. *Young children* can be a mixed blessing. Sometimes they are a joy and a delight; at other times they create problems of loneliness, isolation from friends, boredom and fatigue.

2. *Other women* can be curious creatures. When women look to other women for help, support and friendship, they may at times receive exactly the opposite reactions. Studies reveal that women can be suspicious, jealous, full of gossip, and unfriendly toward one another. A psychologist once explained to us: "Watch out if you are intelligent, good-looking, rich or happy. Others will envy you, others will tell lies about you. Life is not easy."

3. *Your husband* was once your sweetheart and your best friend. You enjoyed his attention, tenderness and love. What made the magic disappear?

Truly, better days are ahead for mothers who learn to value themselves. How can you accomplish this?

- Realize that you are important—you have real value.

- Respect yourself, then others will respect you, too.

- Cultivate interests, friends and meaningful work (either within your home, or outside your home).

- If others ignore you and put you down, search for new friends who will appreciate your kindness and your love.

- Be forgiving. Be patient. Be loving.

Finally, if you are a mother returning to the work-a-day world, we would like to tell you a story which was told to us, not long ago:

"I was so excited! I was going to have lunch with my boss! I prayed that I could talk on an adult level and not act like a child or a teenager.

You see, this had been my world for a very long time. Really, I amazed myself! I really had a great time and I held up my end of the conversation very well!

"When lunch was over, he looked at me rather strangely. Then I realized what I had done. All during lunch, I had been cutting up his steak for him and wiping his face with my napkin! How horrible!"

Yes, mothers make mistakes; but they also deserve forgiveness. Do you agree?

34

Exciting Expressions!

Our subject is "Manners!" The word itself conjures up curious thoughts in this writer's mind. One pictures little girls in lacy dresses, white gloves and shiny, black shoes, smiling on cue and performing dainty curtsies. Or, somewhere in the dark recesses of time and space, one might have a dim vision of a gentleman tipping his hat to a lady or offering her a seat on the subway or saying, "I'm sorry," when something went wrong.

Please understand, we are not suggesting a return to the 1890's, nor are we unrealistic people, searching for Utopia or a pot of gold at the rainbow's end. But we do feel quite sad and discouraged about the lack of manners among the young and the old alike.

Jane Austen, the English novelist, wrote: "Captain Harville, though not equaling Captain Wentworth in manners, was a perfect gentleman." Indeed, between 1775 and 1817, manners were so important that novelists compared and ranked the politeness of story characters! In reading a few current novels, we are amazed at the change of pace. Truly, we have traveled from the sublime to the spicy!

How can we teach good manners to children today? Do you feel that there is a need for more "thank you's" in our world? If you answer "yes," we hope you will read on.

The Matter Is Manners!

Children learn good manners as soon as they learn to listen and to talk. When they hear Mom and Dad speaking politely to each other, then their environment is excellent for acquiring courtesy in speech. If parents teach refined language to their sons and daughters, they are investing in their children's positive development and growth. They are giving them the upper edge in climbing the leadership ladder.

Let us consider now a few gracious words which can make a great difference for boys and girls. Some call them "magic words," but we would like to name them "Exciting Expressions!" They can open many doors, they can change the world!

Thank you—Two little words which two-year-olds can learn to say when receiving a cookie, getting a push on a swing or enjoying a delicious dinner. A mother once told us, "If they say 'thank you' at age two, they are off to a good start!"

Writing thank-you notes is also an important part of successful parenting. Yes, it may be a chore to write thank-you notes to friends and relatives who send us gifts at Christmas time, birthday time or special occasion time, but it is mannerly; it is polite; it is important!

Please—This six-letter word, pronounced with a smile and a pleasing eye, can move mountains! A three-year-old who says, *"Please may I have a drink of water?"* is well on his or her way to the executive office! By contrast, children who live in a "Give me, give me, give me" world are later shunned, not listened to and rejected by peers and bosses.

"Please" means: I respect your feelings, I will not take things without your permission and I need your help.

I'm sorry—Yes, I'm sorry that you're sick, I'm sorry that I hurt you, I'm sorry that I can't be with you today.

"I'm sorry" means that I care about you. It may also tell another person that we made a mistake and we want to say so.

Excuse me, please—I stepped on your toe or I misunderstood you or I interrupted you when you were speaking. "Excuse me, please" means that we seek forgiveness, we wish to be excused for something we did which was wrong.

Fathers and mothers who are quite brave say, "Excuse me, please" to their sons and daughters when they (the parents) have been wrong. This is the way that children acquire manners. They listen carefully to the language of their parents.

Actually, the fruit doesn't fall very far from the tree!

35

They March to the Tune of New Pipers

She has not been home for over a year. Mysteriously, she disappeared one day and left no note, no goodbye, no clue as to where she was going. She is nineteen years old, the daughter of well-to-do, highly educated parents, but she ran away from it all to join a "cult."

Yes, Jennifer, (not her real name) along with many other teenagers and young adults, is marching to the tune of new pipers. Young people are being persuaded, enticed and coaxed into joining the ranks of the cult lifestyle. Why do they leave family, church groups, school, neighborhood and friends? How are they tempted? From what are they running away?

The Lure of the Cult Culture

1. *The need for love.* The breakdown of the American family through divorce, unemployment, scandal and drugs creates a great void in

the lives of young people. They desperately long for their independence, but they crave love and acceptance, too.

When conflicts arise between parent and child, many mothers and fathers put aside their warmth and love and play the role of the authoritarian parent or the policeman or the unbending schoolmaster. So when young people join cults, they feel that they are moving from a negative, non-caring, non-loving family environment to one which espouses non-belligerence and the use of persuasion rather than force. (Such persuasion, however, is only a tactic to lure the young people in—and then things change for the worse.)

2. *The need for spirituality*. A deep spiritual longing and commitment dwells in the hearts of not a few teenagers. When they realize that their parents are not committed to any particular spiritual beliefs, these young people go in search of a religion that offers meaning and structure. Therefore, a cult is quite appealing to those who have no religion within the home.

3. *The need for security*. Child abuse, which can be both physical and verbal, robs youngsters of their feelings of security within the home environment. A cult can be a haven of security where there is promise of no more fighting, nagging or swearing.

4. *The need to be different*. People are "different" when they are taking drugs, "different" when they become promiscuous, and "different" when they run away. Some young people crave so strongly to be unlike their parents that the cult lifestyle is a way for them to detach themselves from parental values and develop a vastly new way of life.

5. *The need for attention*. We all enjoy attention, recognition and acceptance. When children do not receive this type of nurturing and caring at home, they search for it elsewhere. The cult group smiles at them and welcomes them warmly.

6. *The need to be employed*. In our tight job market today, young adults fear the trauma and economic hardship of unemployment. They graduate from high school or college and find themselves desperately searching for a fulfilling career. With few skills related to the job market, they accept dead-end positions which are frustrating and boring, with no chance of advancement. Therefore, when the Unification Church, a Hare Krishna group or any other cult offers free meals, a home and a chance to move up into the hierarchy of the cult, these young men and women look upon this as a career opportunity.

If your child is a preschooler, an elementary-school-age child, a teenager or a young adult—

how do you feel about "children and cults?" Would you want your son or daughter to leave the warmth and love of your family circle and run away, become brainwashed and never be seen again?

In answering the above questions, many parents have decided to try to improve their parenting skills. They have worked diligently to make the home environment one of caring, concern and love. And as we gaze around our dinner table, let us be thankful to God for our families, united together in peace. Let us pray for these runaway children who have left their families and friends. Let us be hopeful that families will be given the grace to become strong and true. For, if we can stitch and sew each American family "back together again," truly, we can mend the fabric of our nation, too!

36

Let's Close Some Doors!

Have you ever heard a wise saying that kept repeating itself in your mind? Perhaps it seemed like a familiar refrain, echoing and then fading away, or maybe you called it "old wine in new bottles." Grandpa might have said, "It's an old chestnut!"

One such sage rhyme is the topic for this chapter. It bravely pronounces:

> *I slammed the door on yesterday*
> *And threw the key away!*
> *Tomorrow holds great joy for me*
> *For I have found my way!*

Do you have some doors to close in your life? Do you have some keys to toss away? Maybe you lost your job or your dear friend or both. Possibly you were recently divorced, separated or widowed. Or, are you the victim of an illness, an accident or alcoholism? There are so many doors to barricade in our family lives. We need to look forward, not backward; we need to turn our eyes toward the sun, not the fog; the warmth, not the cold; the stars, not the mud.

Yet it becomes difficult, sometimes almost impossible, to "slam the door on yesterday." We hear people say: "But, I still love him and I can't forget him." Or, "They were mean to me; I still remember the way they fired me. I can't forget it." And also, "She was a beautiful, teenage girl, and now she's gone, gone forever."

Truly, it is tough. It is not fair. Our emotions will not listen to our mind. That is why the previous poem came to be. The poet wrote it in an attempt to help herself and hopefully a few others, too. At times, we *must* throw the key away. It is our only hope to find a good life again. We must forget the past and look ahead to better days.

Does tomorrow hold great joy for you? How does one find joy when surrounded by tears and worries and turmoil? How do we "find our way"?

The answer to all of this lies in one word. This word began to glimmer and shine about two thousand years ago in a place called Bethlehem.

The messenger and carrier of this small word was called a Teacher and a Master and He came to deliver the Good News of His Father.

How can a word which was given forth so long ago be of value today? What is this word?

The word is called LOVE; it transcends all time and space; it brings great joy; it came down from our Father in heaven.

But, whom should we love? The answer is quite simple. We should love God...ourselves ...and other people.

When we learn to love God, love ourselves and love other people, it becomes so much easier to slam those doors which are paneled with heartache and grief.

How does loving God pertain to throwing keys away? Well, first we must understand Him and His Good News. It is very difficult to love what we do not know.

Therefore, by reading the Scriptures, praying, attending Mass, receiving the sacraments, watching or listening to religious programming on television or radio and reading religious publications, we learn about God's ways and God's plan for our lives.

To begin each morning by silently saying, "I can do all things through Christ who strengthens me," is a good way to show our love and faith in God. It is also an important part of "throwing keys away."

Next, we must try to love ourselves. We must take good care of our body, mind and soul; we must value ourselves as children of God. We are His messengers here on earth. We can find much joy and happiness—even in times of great suffering and pain—when we realize our important mission. Christ wants us to love ourselves so that we can spread His love to others. Remember the song: "Let there be peace on earth and let it begin with me."

Finally, we must love other people. Even when they ignore us and do not return our love, we must still love them. For when we turn our thoughts, words and actions toward helping others, we have truly "found our way!" ...And this is the way in which the kingdom of God can come to us now—and forevermore!

Raising children is...

    exciting
      loving
        wonderful
          difficult
            challenging

If you have any comments after reading this book, we would be delighted to hear from you. Our address is:

Mr. and Mrs. John F. Murphy
4 Camelot Drive
Hingham, MA 02043

Daughters of St. Paul

IN MASSACHUSETTS
50 St. Paul's Ave., Jamaica Plain, Boston, MA 02130; **617-522-8911.**
172 Tremont Street, Boston, MA 02111; **617-426-5464; 617-426-4230.**

IN NEW YORK
78 Fort Place, Staten Island, NY 10301; **212-447-5071; 212-447-5086.**
59 East 43rd Street, New York, NY 10017; **212-986-7580.**
625 East 187th Street, Bronx, NY 10458; **212-584-0440.**
525 Main Street, Buffalo, NY 14203; **716-847-6044.**

IN NEW JERSEY
Hudson Mall—Route 440 and Communipaw Ave.,
Jersey City, NJ 07304; **201-433-7740.**

IN CONNECTICUT
202 Fairfield Ave., Bridgeport, CT 06604; **203-335-9913.**

IN OHIO
2105 Ontario Street (at Prospect Ave.), Cleveland, OH 44115;
216-621-9427.
25 E. Eighth Street, Cincinnati, OH 45202; **513-721-4838;
513-421-5733.**

IN PENNSYLVANIA
1719 Chestnut Street, Philadelphia, PA 19103; **215-568-2638.**

IN VIRGINIA
1025 King Street, Alexandria, VA 22314; **703-683-1741; 703-549-3806.**

IN FLORIDA
2700 Biscayne Blvd., Miami, FL 33137; **305-573-1618.**

IN LOUISIANA
4403 Veterans Memorial Blvd., Metairie, LA 70002; **504-887-7631;
504-887-0113.**
1800 South Acadian Thruway, P.O. Box 2028, Baton Rouge, LA 70821;
504-343-4057; 504-381-9485.

IN MISSOURI
1001 Pine Street (at North 10th), St. Louis, MO 63101; **314-621-0346;
314-231-1034.**

IN ILLINOIS
172 North Michigan Ave., Chicago, IL 60601; **312-346-4228;
312-346-3240.**

IN TEXAS
114 Main Plaza, San Antonio, TX 78205; **512-224-8101; 512-224-0938.**

IN CALIFORNIA
1570 Fifth Ave., San Diego, CA 92101; **619-232-1442.**
46 Geary Street, San Francisco, CA 94108; **415-781-5180.**

IN WASHINGTON
2301 Second Ave., Seattle, WA 98121.

IN HAWAII
1143 Bishop Street, Honolulu, HI 96813; **808-521-2731.**

IN ALASKA
750 West 5th Ave., Anchorage, AK 99501; **907-272-8183.**

IN CANADA
3022 Dufferin Street, Toronto 395, Ontario, Canada.

IN ENGLAND
199 Kensington High Street, London W8 63A, England.
133 Corporation Street, Birmingham B4 6PH, England.
5A-7 Royal Exchange Square, Glasgow G1 3AH, England.
82 Bold Street, Liverpool L1 4HR, England.

IN AUSTRALIA
58 Abbotsford Rd., Homebush, N.S.W. 2140, Australia.